The End of Certainty and the Beginning of Faith

Religion and Science for the 21ˢᵗ Century

D. Brian Austin

SMYTH&
HELWYS

Smyth & Helwys Publishing, Inc.
6316 Peake Road
Macon, Georgia 31210-3960
1-800-747-3016

Library of Congress Cataloguing-in-Publication Data

Austin, D. Brian.
   The end of certainty and the beginning of faith:
   religion and science for the 21st century/
   D. Brian Austin.
   p.   cm.
   Includes bibliographical references and index.
   (alk. paper)
   1. Certainty. 2. Faith. 3. Religion and science. I. Title.
   BD171 .A87 2000
   121'.63—dc21

                                                        99-056444
                                                        CIP

ISBN 1-57312-262-9

Contents

Acknowledgements

Whatever may be of value in these pages is made possible because of the incredible generosity, expertise, forbearance, and cooperation of many persons. Good-natured and skilled student workers Jason Combs, David Brewer, Christy Cobb, Cindy Bright, and Michael Newton contributed greatly to many phases of this project. Secretarial professionalism that astounds her co-workers characterizes the work of Mrs. Pat Brown, who tirelessly treads through the reams of paper I heap upon her, thus making me look a lot better to the outside world. To Pat I owe a special portion of gratitude. Thanks also to Mark McElroy and Jackie Riley of Smyth & Helwys for their support and encouragement, expertise, and patience. Special thanks are due to Dr. Don H. Olive and Dr. John S. Brachey, Jr., who read large portions of the manuscript and made enormously helpful comments, saving me from saying many things that I did not wish to say and from a number of inadvertent omissions. I continue to be grateful to Bonnie, Tom, Lee, Viola, and Vivian for decades of unconditional and often unrequited support, and to David and Seth, for whom I hope to do as well. Finally, and most of all, I thank my wife, Sandra, who stands behind, beneath, and beyond any project I undertake, and whose grace warms and nurtures as it draws a picture of how things should be. The shortcomings in these pages are evidences of my not yet seeing that picture clearly, and, of course, are mine alone.

Introduction

In graduate school I occasionally played golf with a sincere Christian physician. One day he was particularly animated as we approached the first tee at Seneca Golf Course in Louisville, Kentucky. His buoyancy that day resulted from a television show he had watched the night before in which archaeologists had discovered the "actual Ark of the Covenant," that long-lost repository of Hebrew holy relics. "Finally," he said, "we have proof that the Bible is true. Scientific, incontrovertible proof." Undoubtedly the television show featured interviews with scientists wearing white lab coats, the costume of authority that has replaced ecclesiastical vestments for many in the modern age.

Science and religion desperately need to talk to each other, but the above conversation is precisely not the kind of discourse that will promote the legitimate aims of either because the conversation so lauded by the earnest doctor is one that assumes the possibility of achieving certainty. Throughout much of the modern period of Western history—roughly 1600 to 1900 CE—many scientists and philosophers thought that the methods of science, which made very profitable use of logic and mathematics, could, at least in theory, yield indubitable conclusions about any number of perennial human questions of truth, goodness, God, and more. The contemporary period—late nineteenth century through the present—has dashed these hopes. Insights from philosophy and science in this period are painting a picture of a very uncertain world, one that does not neatly obey the mathematical equations used to describe it, one that may not even have the kinds of answers for which we have been seeking. More and more it looks like we have been asking the wrong kinds of questions, demanding from our world information that it does not possess in the first place. Like Job before the whirlwind, the chaotic vortex seems to be telling us that we couldn't understand the answers anyway because we have yet to identify the questions.

Our knowledge of the universe is uncertain, and incontrovertibly so, because all knowledge claims contain reference to an unformed and open future. This unknowable future puts our human projects at great risk, so any courageous engagement of that future requires faith, a commitment to things hoped for but not seen. The universe of chance and risk described by much contemporary science and philosophy is, therefore, an ideal arena for the exercise of a robust faith.

Dreams of finding certainty in claims about God, goodness, life, death, and the universe die hard. From the halls of scientific research centers we hear "proofs" that evolution has defeated Christianity. From denominational headquarters and a thousand pulpits we hear that "God said it, I believe it, and that settles it." Or, in another illicit rendezvous of scientific and religious impulses, we hear that a new Bible translation will achieve some kind of linguistic precision with the aid of "sophisticated computer technology to check the accuracy of meaning in each word."[1] Or we read in an otherwise excellent book about the wondrous intricacies of molecular biology that the "Epic of Evolution" is "how things are," and that this story alone "has the potential to unite us, because it happens to be true."[2]

Large segments of the religious and scientific worlds have yet to come to grips with the end of certainty. The picture drawn by contemporary physics and philosophy discussed in these pages will only fit very loosely, if at all, the universe we seek to describe. It is a world shot through with chance events, with risk, with the indeterminate, with enormous complexity and unpredictability. We cannot hope to squeeze the world into our predefined conceptual categories. There can be no "precise" translation of this messy and uncertain world into the restrictive and clean language that characterizes most mathematics and logic. We will not find the equations that would yield the long-term precise predictability dreamed of by the early moderns. And formulations of religious dogma that have borrowed the rhetoric and the method of modern certainty seekers will fare no better.

The bulk of the pages that follow can be seen as a philosophical tour of some of the highlights in the history of certainty, from its bold beginnings of high hopes to its decline and fall in the twentieth century. The implications of the end of certainty for Christian belief will be broached, especially with regard to the meaning of faith in a world of risk and uncertainty. "Faith" will be treated quite generically in the hopes of providing a jumping-off point for more specific and detailed theological analysis and because this work is primarily philosophical rather than theological.

Standard doctrines of systematic theology will not be addressed here. Though the end of certainty has much to say to the doctrines of God, creation, atonement, salvation, eschatology, and the rest, such a treatment will have to wait.

Chapters 1–4 focus on a series of philosophical problems that began to challenge the dreams of certainty almost from the beginning. Chapters 5–8 examine important scientific discoveries of the twentieth century in light of their impact on certainty and on the life of faith. Chapters 9 and 10 show some ways in which the end of certainty is very good news for people of faith.

The end of certainty and its implications have been noticed and commented upon by a wide array of thinkers from distinct perspectives. I hope that the reader can get a sense that the worldview suggested here has the potential of being developed as a comprehensive picture, transcending the boundaries of science or theology or any other discipline. With flashes of light from a variety of vantage points, the shape of this worldview should slowly resolve itself. Along the way I also hope that the reader might find one or two helpful suggestions about how a Christian might respond to specific questions and challenges that science puts to the believer.

The repeated refrain of the reflections that follow is the philosophy of American thinker Charles Sanders Peirce (1839–1914). The reader will not get even an introduction to Peirce's thought, but if I can convey even a taste of this remarkable thinker's original contributions to philosophy, then an important service will have been rendered, for Peirce's philosophy may give us a key to unlock a rewarding and courageous passageway through this world of uncertainty. The messy and unpredictable world of nature affirmed by so much contemporary science and philosophy appears to many to be a threat to important elements of the Christian faith. But the philosophical notions of Peirce help us to see the affirmations of chance, risk, embodiedness, and openness as beneficial to the essentials of the life of faith.

Though Peirce was not an orthodox Christian—there is considerable debate about the nature of any religious convictions he held—he developed a vision of the world that is remarkably consonant with belief in a personal creator God. At the same time Peirce was a practicing scientist and tireless advocate of the scientific method. Thus in his thought we find a vision of knowledge and reality that is respectful of the best thinking in both religion and science. But we also find more than that because in a worldview that is respectful of both arenas of the human attempt to find truth and meaning, we may well also begin to see a way to reconcile both sides of what has become a major cultural divide in the contemporary Western world.

The impersonal, goal-free, and "value-free" orientation that set modern science apart from its medieval predecessors has been blamed for the eventual secularization of the West. If science can explain nature precisely and potentially exhaustively without recourse to notions of plan, goal, or direction, then what place is there for talk of a God who made the world for a purpose and guides it toward a meaningful goal?

It does seem clear that "scientization" and secularization have occurred hand in hand over the last 200 to 300 years. Contemporary society, though, is witnessing a powerful backlash against any attempts at "value-free" accounts of the world. As a result, there is a growing mistrust of the intelligentsia, a group of persons often portrayed as radical relativists, believing in nothing. In avoidance of this ultimately self-defeating relativism, many have chosen a rather dogmatic recoil, resisting scientific thinking altogether. A Peircean interpretation of contemporary science's picture of an uncertain and fuzzy world may well provide a very promising path between the two extremes of relativism and dogmatism. This view of the world takes science very seriously, but denies that its explanations are either complete or that they tell the only story that can meaningfully bring people together. This view of the world also takes the commitments of faith very seriously and sees them as not substantially distinct from the claims of science. But the fuzziness and uncertainty that have decimated science's dreams of certainty must be allowed to have the same effect on religious beliefs that claim for themselves the kind of certainty denied to science.

The view of the world suggested in the ensuing pages is radically open. It suggests that all of our knowledge and belief is fuzzy and uncertain precisely because the future is open. Our convictions in the present, which I will show to be given content by their orientation toward the future, are fuzzy, messy, and uncertain. We are embodied, changing, developing beings who are trying to learn about the world into which we will cast ourselves for as many tomorrows as we are granted. As such, we cannot hope to attain a disembodied and objective view of the world into which we are inextricably woven. Humans are the chief exemplification of the uncertain world, not the lone exception.

This embodied and future-directed status of persons in a world that is developing right along with us creates an ideal staging ground for faith. Commitment means something if it must withstand the unknown, the chancy future that none of us foresees. A world that is essentially a complex equation or a predetermined script might excite cool assent or even admiration, but not the passionate sacrifice of a self in a way that might actually make a difference. The world described in the following pages, described through a Peircean lens that sees tremendous value in the scientific and the spiritual, is a world in which our lives may be meaningfully surrendered in faith to the service of God, a sacrifice that really does make a difference.

Notes

[1]Officials of Broadman & Holman Publishers cited in *Baptist and Reflector* 165, no. 19 (12 May1999) 2.

[2]Ursula Goodenough, *The Sacred Depths of Nature* (New York: Oxford University Press, 1998) xvi. I am in sympathy with the vast majority of this book, but find this particular overstatement emblematic of a mistaken modernist insistence that scientific modes of thought reveal literal truths and are sufficient even to ground meaning.

The Rise and Fall and Persistence of Certainty

One of the disturbing things about philosophy courses is that the answers are not in the back of the book. There is something comforting about checking your answers against the correct ones listed by the author. Mathematics and logic are two disciplines that often have these correct answers at the end. Introductory courses in these fields have unambiguous methods and results that can be stated accurately and briefly. Courses in philosophy and theology, by contrast, seem mired in dispute even about how to begin. Thousands of philosophers and theologians seem to have poked and prodded the same riddles from a thousand different angles, only to end up proposing a thousand different solutions. Wouldn't it be nice to attack these stubborn riddles with the tools that yield real answers? What a marvelous season would arrive if we could only probe life, death, the heavens, and the earth with the precise tools of mathematics and logic! Thus could we steer a confident course toward a future whose contours would be revealed ahead of time. If nature would only submit to math, we could find security in numbers. Modern science, that revolution that began in the sixteenth century and has only picked up steam since then, promised to make that dream an actuality.

But our story is not confined to the modern period. Early in humans' history of reflecting on their universe, great thinkers recognized the profound implications of mathematical thinking for everything from farming to salvation. The Pythagorean theorem was widely used to determine dimensions of farm fields, but Pythagoras (and his great admirer Plato) also believed that mathematics revealed deep mysteries of heaven. For Plato, the life of true blessedness was barred to all who lacked mathematical proficiency.[1] Legend tells of many Pythagoreans becoming spiritually devastated and deeply depressed when confronted with the fact that certain quantities defied definitive expression in whole numbers.

Many other great minds in Western history have shared this high regard for mathematics, and its closely related—if not ultimately identical discipline—logic. Philosophy in the medieval period, leading up to the epochal work of Galileo, was dominated by tremendous advances in pure logic. A centuries-long revival of Aristotle's teaching in the Middle Ages secured a prestigious status for pure logic, whose rules and results provided for many an ecstatic moment not unlike those mathematical mountaintops lauded by the ancients.

Enter Galileo, whose fame belies his more enduring contribution to the modern world. That contribution can be seen in another well-known claim of his: ". . . that grand book of nature . . . is written in the language of mathematics, without a knowledge of which one cannot understand a word of it, but must wander about forever as in a maze."[2] This assertion is superficially akin to the Pythagorean concerns. The ancients could not have had a clue about the amazing degree to which natural *processes* could be described by mathematical equations. For Pythagoras and his followers, numbers provided a means for escape from an unsatisfactory world of change and decay. For Galileo, math provided the key to unlock the wonder of creation.

This rigorous application of mathematical functions to physical systems is Galileo's true legacy. He was in this sense the first truly modern physicist, measuring and recording results of experimental processes in precise quantitative terms. Though he probably never dropped heavy objects from the leaning tower of Pisa as legend affirms, he did roll balls of various weights down planes of various inclines and was thereby able to determine a consistent force of attraction downward, regardless of the weight of the ball. He also used thought experiments to demonstrate further that the rate of this downward motion did not depend on the falling body's weight. Simple equations could describe this consistent force. Nature harbored hidden patterns that could only be read and spoken by those fluent in the language of mathematics.

The power of this new method seemed unlimited. What other mysteries of nature could be exposed? What hidden forces could be uncovered? How many perennial problems and questions of humanity could now be solved? Galileo and many contemporaries believed that they had hit upon a method that could provide myriad solutions to countless conundrums. They were right, and no one saw this more clearly than René Descartes. Because religious institutions seemed only to stand in the way of the march toward new and certain knowledge, it seemed best to carry on the scientific work out of earshot of the bishops. If they insisted on playing by the old, outdated rules, then the moderns would simply start a new game, to whose victors belong the spoils, a powerful and fruitful kind of certainty.

Descartes' Declaration of Certainty

When René Descartes (1596–1650), the father of modern philosophy and analytic geometry, had finished his formal education at La Flèche (outside Paris), he felt that most of his studies had only served to confuse him. He had completed a thorough Jesuit education, one of the best curricula available during his time, but thought that most of it had been worthless. On the issues most important to human beings, the traditional philosophical and theological disciplines had produced only "endless disputations," with each thinker's theory allegedly refuted by someone else's. The only exceptions were in his studies of mathematics and logic, where he found the solace he sought—the solace of certainty.

His unfortunate state of confusion led him to seek diligently for some fact, some piece of knowledge that could not possibly be doubted. His method for this search has become the method known as Cartesian doubt. In order to find something that could not be doubted, he decided to try to doubt everything he had hitherto believed. It was as if he sat alone next to a kind of intellectual trash bin and tossed any belief that was not absolutely certain into that bin. For a while it looked like none of his beliefs would withstand this "dubitability test."

He tossed large portions of what he believed into the bin when he saw that everything his senses had told him may have been a deception.

> Everything I have accepted up to now as being absolutely true and assured, I have learned from or through the senses. But I have sometimes found that these senses played me false, and it is prudent never to trust entirely those who have once deceived us.[3]

There was even the remote possibility that his beloved math and logic might be wrong. It is within the range of possibility, he conjectured, that there is some powerful and cunning superhuman demon whose mission it is to deceive us about even these apparently obvious beliefs. Is there anything left?

Even if a great demon were intent on tricking us, even if we were engaged in a long, strange dream, even if our senses could not be trusted, then there is still someone who is being deceived. Even if all of my beliefs were false, there still has to be a "me" who has all of these false beliefs. In other words, as long as I am thinking, I must be existing. This realization is, of course, Descartes' famous *cogito ergo sum*, "I think, therefore I am." This was the one truth that could not possibly be doubted under any circumstances. He was so certain of this conclusion that "all the most extravagant suppositions of the skeptics were not capable of shaking it."[4] Descartes' declaration created a defining moment for the modern world's fascination with certainty. For from now on, there appeared to be that basic self-evident axiom that is needed for any geometry-style proof. With this foundation established, Descartes thought we could proceed by unassailably logical steps to infer a great number of truths about ourselves, God, and the universe. The Holy Grail was in sight, and it could be grasped with the help of sound deductive reasoning.

If your beginning axiom is certain, and if the inferences drawn from it are carried out within the proper rules of deductive reasoning, then each inference "inherits" the certainty of the premises leading to it. The most often cited model for a deductive argument was used as an example by Aristotle (384–322 BCE) and practically every logic teacher since: "All men are mortal, Socrates is a man, therefore Socrates is mortal." The conclusion, "Socrates is mortal," is established beyond the shadow of a doubt because of the alleged certainty of the two premises and the relationship between them. If the two premises ("all men are mortal" and "Socrates is a man") are true, then clearly there is no way under heaven that the conclusion could be false. And it is likewise obvious, so Aristotle thought, that the premises are true. Descartes was quite impressed with this feature of reasoning, its ability to produce indubitable conclusions. We will return shortly to this alleged indubitability, but for now suffice it to recognize a reason for Descartes' love of logic.

With *cogito ergo sum*, Descartes felt that he had found an unimpeachable logical foundation. From this foundation he would proceed to develop other certainties by the same sort of reasoning that convinces us of Socrates' mortality. Among the first of these other inferences that Descartes drew was the "obvious" claim that he was first and foremost a "thinking thing." This was obvious to him because it was his thinking process alone that was assured existence. The only undoubtedly existing thing was the doubting entity, which was his mind, not his body. The body might, in fact, still be an hallucination; but the mind being deceived must exist in order to be deceived. Thus the existing thing was a thinking thing.

Furthermore, this "thinking thing" seemed to hold some kinds of ideas to be necessarily true. It was "pre-programmed" with ideas that could not be false. Among the most important of these ideas that came "built-in" was the idea of God. But the idea of God was different from other ideas that populated the shelves of the "thinking thing." The idea of God was magnificent, grand, perfect, and infinite. Surely an idea of this magnitude could not have arisen from a cause less perfect than itself. To explain the presence of so sublime a notion as that of God, a God was required. The only way this idea could exist in the mind of the human was if God had expressly put it there. In case this isn't convincing evidence for the existence of God, Descartes reached back in history to update an older, though still purely conceptual, argument for God's existence. This argument contends that the very definition of "God" that exists in the mind of the thinking self attributes to God the maximum of all perfections. Among these perfections that define the concept of God is the quality of really existing. As the most perfect being, God *must* exist, since lacking existence would be imperfect. An existing God is more perfect than an imaginary God, so the content of the idea of God in the human mind necessitates the actual existence of this God.

God's existence, to Descartes, could be believed with exactly the same certainty that accompanied the *cogito* itself, and this implied even more. Since God necessarily possessed the maximum of all perfections, then, unlike the conjectural deceiving demon from before, God could not make a habit of deception. Trustworthiness is a perfection, so God is maximally trustworthy. Hence the really obvious, or "clear and distinct," ideas accepted by humans could generally be trusted, too. After all, God would not endow God's highest creation with faulty intellectual faculties. Now this does not mean that we can automatically trust every impression we have, since we are clearly finite and imperfect creatures, but in those cases where we are overwhelmed with the clarity and distinctness of some notion, we can count on that notion.

So René Descartes has come full circle. Earlier he had discarded every belief he held as being uncertain. The intellectual trash bin was full. But his revelation of the *cogito* had assured him, after a couple of valid deductions from it, that much of what his mind and his senses had told him was true after all. So the trash could be recycled, reclaimed, and reused—which, of course, means that it is not really trash after all, though we cannot see its value until we have proven God's existence.

Descartes gloried in this certainty. After applying his geometrical method to a variety of problems, he concluded,

> Not only did I resolve several questions which I had earlier judged to be very difficult, but it also seemed to me, towards the end, that I could determine, even in those of the solution of which I was ignorant, by what means and how far it would be possible to resolve them. In this I shall not perhaps appear to you to be too vain, if you consider that, as there is only one truth of each thing, whoever finds it knows as much about the thing as there is to be known.[5]

Descartes' newfound method promised certain solutions to humankind's most intractable difficulties. Questions regarding human nature, God's nature, ethics, science, metaphysics, and more could now be profitably explored, with a realistic hope of attaining answers that could not seriously be doubted. The answers *were* in the back of the book after all; we just had to learn the language in which the book was written. Descartes agreed with Galileo that language is mathematical. In addition to being the father of modern philosophy, Descartes is also considered the father of analytic geometry, a discipline that has either inspired or scandalized millions who have been taught to represent nature on the "Cartesian" coordinate plane. Descartes thought there was no reason why the precision of geometrical thinking might not be applied to any and all philosophical difficulties. Modern science was up and running, beginning a revolution in human thinking, and it held the potential to accomplish nothing less than the relief of the human condition.

Little did Descartes suspect that the very method by which he had reached his hopes of certainty contained the very seeds of the demise of that hope. To give away a bit of the end of the story, the Cartesian "thinking thing," confidently discovered at the end of his doubting program, is so separate and distinct from the objects it would know that a practically unbridgeable gulf had been created between the knower and the known.

Hume's Demolition of Certainty

One of English philosopher John Locke's (1632–1704) primary missions was to inject a bit of humility into what appeared to be an overconfident continental European philosophy. The success of his efforts would probably have shocked him, had he lived to see it. Rather than seeing the mind as a repository of pre-programmed axiomatic truths, Locke explicitly described the mind prior to sense experience as *tabla rasa*, or "blank slate." In other words, any knowledge of the world that humans possess must arrive by way of the senses. Locke was not original in affirming this empiricist teaching—it goes back to the ancient Stoics—but his penetrating analysis of the processes and implications of this method of knowing was unique and momentous. As natural as this theory of knowing sounds to most Westerners, it harbors a potentially fatal flaw, especially if wedded to an essentially Cartesian view of the self as detached ego.

If my mind must absorb knowledge from its surroundings, then it is never the object of knowledge itself that enters my mind, but only a representation of it. And because representations are all I can have in my mind, there can be no assured means of checking the accuracy of those representations. If there is any checking to be done, then this can only be accomplished by other representations. There is no way to test my mental images against a real world outside my mind, because only the images populate my psyche. A person cannot compare his or her ideas against a reality external to the mind, because one cannot know of anything external to the mind. I can report my psychological states to you ("I see a truck coming"), and you can report yours to me ("I've been hit by a truck"), but whether these reports are accurate in some "objective" sense seems an unapproachable issue.

We can even check with another witness (of whom we also know only representations), who might say "Oh my! You've been hit by a truck." In this statement they might seem to be confirming our previous representations of the event, increasing our confidence that our psychological experiences of a truck accident correspond to some "real" event. What this corroborating testimony really claims is that there seems to be a sort of connectedness between a number of different impressions or experiences. My seeing the truck coming, and your sensation of pain of being injured by a collision, and the report of the witness all seem to be connected. This connection is called "reality" or "world" or "fact." Locke's big problem, expressed incisively by David Hume (Scottish philosopher, 1711–1776), is explaining how we can form a representation of this "connection."

You feel the impact of the truck upon your knee and thigh, followed immediately by severe pain. Because of previous experiences of the impact-pain correlation, you surmise that the truck has caused the pain. But, given that all human knowledge must be based upon sense impressions, wherein lies the sense impression of the connection? You experience the impact, then the pain. Did you experience the causal link between them? The *tabla rasa* true believer's answer can only be "no" because the connection between two impressions cannot itself *be* an impression. *Tabla rasa* seems impotent to supply a good reason to affirm a connection.

Maybe the example of seeing a pin bursting a rubber balloon will more clearly illustrate the difficulty. Many times we have seen the results of an encounter between a pin and a balloon. The sharp point makes contact with the rubber skin, and the skin ruptures, the balloon bursts. Let us focus our attention at that moment of contact between pin and skin. We have a visual experience of the pin touching the balloon, followed closely by a visual and auditory experience as the balloon pops. Did our senses record the connection between these two experiences? Clearly they did not. We had experience "A" (contact) and then experience "B" (bang!). Why do we think there is some connection between these experiences? To Hume, it is the force of habit. Whenever we have seen things like "A," we see (and hear) things like "B." So we form a habit of expecting B's to follow A's. We normally jump to the conclusion that there is something about the makeup of the world that necessitates B's following A's. It is precisely this jump that Hume interrogates. He concludes that we have no reason to believe that anything about the world requires that these experiences be correlated.

If he is right, then the implications are staggering for the modern view of knowledge. The implications are great because it seems that any significant human claim of knowledge has the precise structure of describing just the kinds of connections that are so problematic. If one claims that something about the nature of the universe dictates that pins normally pop balloons, that the sun normally rises in the east, that humans perish when they inhale sufficient amounts of water, and so on, then one is claiming that events are tied together in some way. If my impressions of these events are the only possible contents of my mind, then I can possess no significant knowledge. The fact that force of habit has us presume a connection is no reason to claim knowledge of that connection or the world that it may imply. Just because each prior experience of a certain type has certain characteristics is no reason to believe that subsequent experiences of that type will have the same characteristics. Just because gravity seems to attract with a consistent force in the tiny regions of the universe where our measurements can be carried out is no reason to presume that the same consistency would be evident in regions where we have not measured.

This collection of difficulties is generally known as the "problem of induction," and it provided (and continues to provide) a powerful challenge to Descartes' declaration of certainty about knowledge of the world. Not only can we not be certain of any claim made about the world of experience, but also according to Hume's theory we cannot know anything of this world.

Hume did, however, admit that there were kinds of claims that could not be wrong. These kinds of statements Hume called "relations of ideas." In general, Hume placed the "truths" of mathematics and logic in this category. These claims, if true, have the characteristic of being necessarily true; they cannot be imagined to be false at all. Unfortunately, these claims are entirely uninformative about any actual state of affairs. Statements such as "circles are round" and "triangles have three sides" and "bachelors are unmarried" would all be relations of ideas in Hume's scheme. Notice that none of these sentences contributes any information about any world. It is part of the definition of circles that they be round, of triangles that they have three sides, and of bachelors that they be unmarried. In a sense, these definitions are arbitrary. Convention has decided that these terms will bear certain meanings; hence they do. Nowhere do they reveal anything about actually existing bachelors, triangles, or circles.

All widgets are frumptious. All frumptious things have nargles. Hence, widgets have nargles. These three sentences clearly represent a valid piece of deductive reasoning. If the first two are true, then the third is necessarily true. But are the first two claims, the premises, really true? They are if we agree that "widgets" are defined as necessarily "frumptious" and that "frumptiousness" requires the presence of "nargles." In other words, these terms only take on meaning as I, or we, arbitrarily decide those meanings. Some person or persons sets up the rules of the discourse game, and we agree to use those rules. Do the statements in this game have anything to do with anything outside the games whose rules we have created? It seems impossible to show it, if they do. So if we declare that widgets are frumptious, then they are. If we define "bachelors" as unmarried men, then they are. In neither case have we said anything about a world outside our own mental world of concept manipulation.

Comedian Bill Cosby used to perform a stand-up routine that highlights Hume's point about these relations of ideas. In his piece called "Kindergarten," he relates with great enthusiasm his first day of first grade. There the teacher instructs the students that "one plus one equals two." The children are thrilled with this first math lesson and repeat energetically to the teacher, "one and one make two" over and over again. Then they pause in apparent revelatory confusion, "Hey, what's a two?" There is a sense in which David Hume—and many thinkers after him—wondered the same thing.

Yes, our systems (languages) of mathematics and logic yield conclusions that are certain (1+1=2), but is there any indication in this language that it describes any actually existing objects? Even Plato wondered about the mystery of determining whether any given thing is singular, multiple, or fractional.[6] The math works fine, but how, exactly, does it apply to anything outside our minds? Is math anything more than the examination of relations between ideas, a complex analysis of widgets, nargles, and frumptiousness? Hume seems to think not. It is a clever system, a very complicated and enjoyable game, like chess; but it doesn't tell us anything for sure about the universe in which we must live. If there are parallels between our conceptual world and the world of nature, then there is no way to show that these parallels are anything but accidental. Within the rules of chess some moves are clearly legal, and some are not. Nothing can dictate to us, though, that we must continue to play that game. The rules of chess cannot require that the contestants continue to play chess. In real war, rules are abandoned. So chess bears only a very loose resemblance to the actual conditions of combat.

Similarly, logic and mathematics have their own patterns and rules. But how do we know if these rules apply to anything outside the game? The rules are strict and uncompromising, but must they be followed? And what do they have to do with the real world? Hume seemed to think that they could not be shown to apply at all, except to indicate patterns that roughly describe the experiences we have already had. Since these reports can tell us nothing about those regions of reality we have not yet experienced, we must remain totally agnostic about the undiscovered country that lies ahead.

Inductive reasoning, which requires among other things the accumulation of data, seeks to apply the principles of sound logic to the world of experience. But Hume has apparently shown the difficulty of applying habits of the mind to a real physical world. No matter how hard we try to discern the logical patterns of nature, we have no solid reason to conclude that our mental definitions and rules must govern anything outside the game created by those rules. And for Hume, inductive reasoning seems profoundly wrongheaded. According to Hume's way of thinking, what we had hitherto called confident knowledge is nothing other than psychological habit, differing not at all in quality from the habits of thousands of subhuman organisms. Such a reading of human knowledge must surely be wrong, but what is the right one? Hume never claims to have found it. Later we will see that understanding knowledge as habit need not be a demeaning assessment, as Hume's critics presumed. Hume's conclusions, popularized and disseminated through his immensely readable volume *An Enquiry Concerning Human Understanding*, announced a kind of shipwreck of human reason. Hume could not accept Descartes' insertion of built-in indubitables into the human soul, yet the sense-based alternative of Locke's *tabla rasa* seemed to have run aground and spilled its load on rocky shore. Only the unparalleled genius of Immanuel Kant seemed to provide a promising new direction.

Kant's Deferral of Certainty

German philosopher Immanuel Kant (1724–1804) was reared in an intellectual tradition closer to that of Descartes than to that of Hume. Kant, early in his career, was a dutiful expositor of the philosophical method he inherited from Gottfried Leibniz (1646–1716) and Christian Wolff (1679–1754). These two predecessors, like Descartes, preferred the method of logical deduction from self-evident axioms. This preference, generally referred to as "rationalism," though initially promising as a method of reaching assured knowledge about a wide range of problems, issued into the rather embarrassing result of each proponent arriving at a very different understanding of the nature of the universe. If this method was supposed to lead to the certainty so boldly proclaimed by Descartes, then why did his conclusions seem so unsatisfactory to rationalist Benedict Spinoza (1632–1677), whose conclusions were likewise unacceptable to fellow rationalist Leibniz? Either the method was being misused, the axioms were not correct, or the method was inadequate.

The young Kant was disturbed by the quagmire in which philosophy on the continent had foundered, but it was not until he read the work of Scotsman David Hume that he began to see a way out. Sometime in the 1770s Kant was exposed to the radical skeptical insights of Hume. From then on Kant, remarkably mature in years for the advent of works of genius, was to write prolifically from his new perspective, forever changing the landscape of Western thought.

Kant set out to save knowledge from the deadly skepticism inherent in the radical empiricism of David Hume. Kant and legions of followers believed that he had succeeded. History has generally concurred that, to the extent he did succeed, he did so only by truncating the meaning of the word "knowledge." Now is not the time for a detailed description of Kant's theory of knowledge, but for the purpose of outlining the decline of certainty, his definition of legitimate knowledge can be paraphrased economically. He viewed knowledge as "sense data as categorized by the understanding." Kant's masterful *Critique of Pure Reason* (1781) presents detailed analyses of how the human mind goes about its remarkable process of collecting and organizing information.

In a sense, Kant's program steers a kind of middle ground between the rationalist notion of the mind as prewired with useful axioms and the empiricists' *tabla rasa*. For Kant, the human understanding prior to the advent of sense experience exists as empty structure, ready to be filled. Often called the "categories" or "grids," this structure is the prerequisite for any experience at all. So the empiricists were wrong in viewing the understanding as a largely passive tablet, merely absorbing the vast number of data pounding in upon it. The rationalists were wrong in thinking that there was any content without the benefit of the senses. For there to be knowledge, there had to be sense data *and* the categories. Rather than a blank tablet, the understanding is rather like a nicely indexed multi-subject notebook at the beginning of a semester. For there to be any useful information recorded in the notebook, it must be indexed.

Another useful analogy might be a library before any books are actually acquired. If one desires to build a library, then an efficient cataloging system is essential. Imagine a library about to start acquiring its books. The shelves will all be in place, marked with Library of Congress subject notations, ready to receive books in the right places. When the books (sense data) come in, they are indexed in a number of different ways and placed in their proper locations. When books are not in their proper location, they are considered lost, and may as well not exist at all. So Kant's view of knowledge demands that the human understanding categorize all sense impressions, indexing them in various ways. Without the indexing and categorizing, the experience is lost, or put more accurately within Kant's framework, it never counted as experience in the first place.

There are at least three important implications of this theory of knowledge for our story of certainty. First, Kant installs an irrevocable contribution of the knower into the act of knowing, seemingly precluding any possibility of objectivity. Second, according to many subsequent thinkers, he places what we would now call "scientific" kinds of knowing in a privileged position. Third, he creates a profound and permanent distinction between the "scientific" modes of knowing and any other kind of human experience. These three outcomes may not even be mutually consistent, nor are they necessarily what Kant intended, but their impact on today's world has been wide and deep.

Different people took different things from Kant. A large group, mostly from the European continent, saw a revolutionary revision of the role of the knower. Since any experience at all must, in order to be an experience, fit into the categories of the knowing subject, it seems that we must admit our utter inability to see anything as it really is. Of necessity, we see things only as perceivable by creatures with the mental categories we take to the encounter. Any potential reality that is not "indexable" by human classification schemes is forever beyond our ability to know. For instance, everything we experience has to happen sometime, somewhere, and for some reason. Is this because reality is so structured by time, place, and cause? No. It is because *we* invariably supply these indexes to any experience that would be an experience. Whether some objective reality has these characteristics is not ours to know. Or, as the deconstructionists would put it, "the thing-in-itself always escapes." Kant himself prefigured this twentieth-century dictum, by consigning questions of the thing-in-itself to the mysterious and unapproachable realm he named "noumena."

Another important post-Kantian stream of thought took solace from his emphasis on the importance of sense data and rigorous categorization. Earlier we said that Kant had truncated the domain of knowledge. Many persons attracted to the obvious successes of the physical sciences see in Kant a privileged position for these sciences and see his narrow boundaries of knowledge as legitimate. If knowledge is seen as sense data categorized by the human understanding, then we should notice what sorts of things cannot be considered the objects of knowledge. Areas of human experience roughly classified as ethical, aesthetic, and religious seem always to fall outside the realm of that which could be known. Since we will never have a direct sense impression of God, of moral goodness, or of beauty itself, we should not seek to classify claims from these areas as knowledge. Feelings and sensations from these areas might be powerful, meaningful, even overwhelming, but they are prohibited from issuing forth knowledge, on Kant's definition. Many thinkers skeptical of the reality of objects in these regions of human experience have used Kant as one weapon to suggest the irrelevance or even emptiness of talk about God or values. We will return to this theme later, but it must be noted that though Kant did exclude these subjects from the class of things we could really know, he thought ethics, aesthetics, and God important enough topics to warrant most of his subsequent philosophical writings.

Though he did write voluminously about values and religious themes, Kant made it clear that our experience in these areas was of a different order than those in the world of sense and understanding. Most interpreters see Kant as endorsing a kind of "moral faith" that made rational space for God and goodness, even though these were among objects that could not strictly be known. For Kant, it seems as if there are fundamentally different faculties at work in the gaining of knowledge and in the experiences of value and religion. The historical importance of this separation is hard to exaggerate. Kant had succeeded in establishing a powerful philosophical argument in support of Galileo's conviction that religion and science are very different kinds of things. We still live with the effects of that separation, and those who would seek to overcome it are faced with a gargantuan task.

One major tradition in Western philosophy has been very happy with Kant's delimitation of knowledge. This movement, generally known as analytic philosophy, dominated English-speaking philosophy for most of the twentieth century. Kant was part of its inspiration because he defined the boundaries of knowledge clearly and persuasively. The analytic thinkers, mostly English speakers, but with some key support from the European continent, sought to continue in a Kantian vein by eliminating from the realm of meaningful discourse any talk of objects that could not be known with precision. Emboldened by the ever-growing successes of the natural sciences, some analytic philosophers developed an almost Cartesian confidence that mathematical precision and certainty could be applied to observations about the natural world. This confidence was to be dashed summarily before the middle of the twentieth century.

Analysis in the Twentieth Century

Much of the early twentieth century's quest for certainty took the form of a quest for the boundaries of the legitimate use of language. Just as Kant had sought to describe those regions of experience about which humans could think clearly, analytic philosophers sought to describe those regions of experience about which humans could speak clearly and meaningfully. Following in Descartes' footsteps of seeking clear and distinct ideas, and

Hume's dictum that all meaningful concepts must be rooted in sense impressions, the analytic thinkers sought to purge from the language of philosophy any utterances that were not directly traceable to clear and distinct sense impressions.

Most analytic thinkers were convinced that the vast majority of philosophical conundrums in history were the result of linguistic confusion. If we really succeeded in using words carefully and precisely, with clear ideas of those objects to which our words refer, then most, if not all, of the ancient mysteries could be solved. Or rather, they would be *dis*solved, since when the problems are shown to be nothing but confused usage of language, we would see that they were not really problems at all. For instance, humans have always wondered about the true nature of moral goodness. From Socrates until now some of our best minds have sought the essence of righteousness. Taking their cue again from Hume, the analytic philosophers might address this issue as follows.

For them, a proper analysis of good and evil requires a review of actual events or actions that have garnered these evaluations. When we happen upon a murder scene, for example, we will be inclined to name the event and its perpetrator as evil. But a close inspection of the encounter reveals no such thing. It reveals a murder weapon, a victim's body, blood, fingerprints, shoeprints, and other evidence, but no evil. Even the microscopic forensic analysis of crime evidence fails to uncover the "badness" of the act. So the words "evil" or "bad" are actually descriptions of the reaction of the person who happens upon this unfortunate scene. It is a human tendency to project our own feelings and judgments into some allegedly objective state of affairs. So the "evil" that we name is but a fiction, if we think that it refers to some objective quality in an event or a person. The only possible content of the expression "evil" is a report of the feeling of repulsion, of extreme disapproval.

When, however, we witness a young child shrieking with glee at the gyrations of a monarch butterfly on a bright spring morning, we name our feeling of approval. We call it "good." This does not apply to any objective feature of the scene, as no careful analysis of the data will reveal a hint of goodness. But we fall prey to the temptation to objectify our own reactions. If we profoundly approve of the toddler-butterfly encounter, then we impute goodness to the event.

Thus the perennial question about the nature of good and evil has been solved by being dissolved. In both of the above scenes there is an event and a strong reaction to the event. There is no need to go beyond analyzing the event and the reaction, since these are the only singular experiences to which our words can legitimately apply. Literally speaking, the words "good" and "bad" refer to nothing, and this human insistence on absolutizing our feelings has simply led to conceptual confusion. Similar analyses have been applied to other philosophically difficult matters, such as God, freedom, beauty, mind, soul, and love. If we could only purify our language of such fictions, then we will be left with concepts and objects that can be clearly defined. And these clearly defined ideas could then be examined and manipulated according to the fixed and immutable laws of logic and mathematics. Much of the history of analytic philosophy, at least until the middle part of the twentieth century, can be seen as a search for this purified kind of language.

Thinkers widely agree that this bold quest failed. Problems at the foundations of mathematics and problems with the consistency and/or completeness of formal symbol systems (such as arithmetic, for example) led most of these radical analytic thinkers to abandon the hope for a purified symbol system (language) that could even theoretically provide hope for a future airtight means of describing what might be the case about the world. The technical details of this failure in analytic philosophy are beyond the scope of this study, but we will examine several other parallel developments that have contributed to the demise of the hopes for this analytic kind of certainty. Some of the most far-reaching of these parallel developments were born from the study of language. Among other things, it was determined that language does much more than simply describe objects to which it refers. Its functions are, in fact, practically endless. Moreover, the objects we seek to describe with words and other symbols keep slipping out of the boundaries created by those words. Chapter 2 will examine in more detail this creative metaphorical slippage.

Notes

[1] See Plato, *The Republic*, 522e.
[2] Quoted in Stillman Drake, *Galileo Studies: Personality, Tradition, and Revolution* (Ann Arbor MI, 1970) 11.
[3] *Discourse on Method and the Meditations*, trans. F. E. Sutcliffe (London: Penguin Books, 1968) 96.
[4] Ibid., 54.
[5] Ibid., 43.
[6] See Plato, *The Republic*, 479b.

For Further Reading

Ayer, A. J. *Language, Truth, and Logic*. New York: Dover Publications Inc., 1952.

Baird, Forrest, and Walter Kaufmann. *Philosophic Classics*. Vol. 3, *Modern Philosophy*. 2d ed. Upper Saddle River NJ: Prentice-Hall, 2000.

Descartes, René. *Discourse on Method and Meditations*. Translated by F. E. Sutcliffe. New York: Penguin Books, 1968.

Devlin, Keith. Goodbye. *Descartes: The End of Logic and the Search for a New Cosmology of the Mind*. New York: John Wiley and Sons, 1997.

Gaukroger, Stephen. *Descartes: An Intellectual Biography*. Oxford: Clarendon Press, 1995.

Hume, David. *An Enquiry Concerning Human Understanding*. Indianapolis: Hackett Publishing Co., 1977.

Stumpf, Samuel Enoch. *Socrates to Sartre: A History of Philosophy*. 4th ed. New York: McGraw-Hill, 1988.

The Myth
of Literality

The quest for certainty that seemed to collapse with the failure of the logical positivist movement in the early twentieth century had already been severely challenged by a number of thinkers. One notable figure who questioned even the ultimate value of trying to find certainty was Søren Kierkegaard, whose notions we will investigate later. But other figures, from very different backgrounds, contributed substantial arguments that questioned the possibility of certainty, around the turn of the century. In this chapter we will examine the remarkably forward-looking theories of France's Henri Bergson, Germany's Friedrich Nietzsche, Britain's Alfred North Whitehead (who later moved to the U. S.), before looking once again to Plato. Then we will see how many of these insights about language and its connection to the physical world were incorporated into the influential philosophy of American Charles Sanders Peirce. The relevant work of these three men was done in a tremendously rich time period of less than fifty years at the end of the nineteenth and beginning of the twentieth century. Because the last chapter concluded with the dashed hopes of one branch of analytic philosophy, we will begin with Bergson, who highlighted the severe limitations of analytical thinking.

Bergson and Analysis

French philosopher Henri Bergson (1859–1941) is now viewed as one of the early proponents of what later came to be known as "process philosophy," a movement primarily associated with Whitehead. Bergson thought that the modern tendency to analyze objects from a scientific, quantitative perspective would never give us an adequate understanding of those objects. He thought it unfortunate that the scientific, analytical model of knowing had become the only acceptable one in many circles. In his insightful little book, *Introduction to Metaphysics* (1903), Bergson suggests that analysis

> is the operation which reduces the object to elements already known, that is, to elements common both to it and other objects. To analyze, therefore, is to express a thing as a function of something other than itself. All analysis is thus a *translation* [my emphasis], a development into symbols, a representation taken from successive points of view from which we note as many resemblances as possible between the new object which we are studying and others which we believe we know already.[1]

His convictions about analysis relate to the positivists' failure to construct a completely clear and unambiguous formalized language that would be fitted onto some world of facts. According to Bergson, any attempt to describe an object using language is necessarily incomplete and uncertain. This is because there is no place to stop in our process of describing; descriptions of any object are potentially infinite. The descriptions are clearly not the object being described. They are a kind of translation. Anyone who has ever worked at translating from one language to another knows that there is no such thing as a perfectly accurate translation. One language never completely captures the meanings of any expression in another language. The only possible exception to this generalization might be with regard to mathematical quantities, whose highly formalized meanings seem independent of the arbitrarily chosen symbols used to represent them, but it seems this formalization gains clarity only at the expense of applicability to the real world. Bergson was concerned with the concrete world of human experience, the one in which we encounter objects outside our own minds and then interact with them.

Of significance for our tour through the history of certainty is Bergson's telling critique of the standard Western model of knowing, which places the knowing subject (you and I) in a birds-eye-view position with regard to the objects it would know. This is why the best kind of knowledge is usually called "objective." Our scientific culture, emboldened (falsely?) by the imposition of mathematics onto natural systems, then persuades us that this "objective" description can be certain and is the best and most complete kind of description possible.

But Bergson would have us look at the process by which we analyze any object, whether it be the oil lamp in front of me or my best friend. Whether the object of analysis is simple or complex, possible "objective" descriptions are endless, and are always given in terms of something outside the object itself. I could describe the lamp to you by reporting its shape (flattened spheroid with a trumpet-shaped top), its color (off-white with fuzzy butterfly shape baked in), and its weight (about five ounces). But this vague report could be made infinitely more precise. Moreover, I have described it only from one perspective. It would be described somewhat differently if the observer were to move slightly, or if the lighting conditions were different, or if the vision of the observer underwent some sort of change. Even a mathematical description is similarly incomplete. With enough effort, one could determine the mathematical formula for the shape of the lamp, give very precise spectrographic data for the colors reflected from each portion of its surface, report its mass in apparently precise terms. But even here there is not complete precision. Any mathematical description will only be accurate to a certain number of decimal places, and the parameters we decide to measure will only be a few of those that we might measure. These minuscule possible sources of imprecision may seem trivial, but we will see later that recent scientific work sees them as anything but trivial. The importance of imperceptibly small inaccuracies is highlighted when the object of analysis is remarkably complex, such as when the object analyzed is a human being.

Furthermore, such descriptions are always a translation. They are attempts to use symbols to represent to our minds something other than the symbols themselves. My experience of the lamp is like the original of a literary work. My attempt to translate that experience into words and concepts has succeeded in giving you some idea of what the lamp is like, but nothing will really substitute for a direct experience of the lamp itself. Our experiences of objects are much richer and fuller than the concepts we employ to think about them and to communicate them. Hence the language we use in these descriptions never describes completely. And our private thoughts, which also employ this language, share the same limitations. These words and thoughts are always partial, biased, and insofar as they seek to be substitutes for the reality itself, at least a little bit wrong.

Nietzsche and the Infinite Object

German philosopher Friedrich Nietzsche is surely an unlikely ally of someone like Henri Bergson, but Nietzsche, in his role as prophet of postmodernism, makes a number of observations that are consonant with Bergson's. In reflecting on the nature of art as imitation, Nietzsche notes art's aim to represent " 'all nature faithfully'—But by what feint can nature be subdued to art's constraint? Her smallest fragment is still infinite! And so he paints but what he likes in it. What does he like? He likes, what he can paint."[2] This idea prefigures those of Bergson, but adds another important point that applies well beyond the realm of aesthetics.

Whether we are seeking to represent reality in pictures or in words, we come to the task with a particular "vocabulary." As E. H. Gombrich (the aesthetician who used the Nietzsche quote above) puts it: "The artist, no less than the writer, needs a vocabulary before he can embark on a 'copy' of reality."[3] Some painters are very good at drawing faces, others have special abilities with limbs and digits, and others prefer not to represent the human form at all. So what kind of picture of the world do we get from any particular artist? We get a picture that features the artist's specific skills. Furthermore, the artist has chosen the subject in the first place based on her abilities in representing different things. The same goes for those who communicate primarily with words. The experiences that my words convey to you can only be described with words that are part of my vocabulary, and they function effectively only if those words are also part of your vocabulary. I choose to describe only those things, and those perspectives on things, for which my vocabulary is adequate.

So are words capable of providing an exact and literal description of any state of affairs, a precise account of the way things are, or the way any particular thing actually is? Can we hope that they will ever guide us to the "one truth concerning any matter" that Descartes thought he could sometimes find? Nietzsche's and Bergson's answers are unequivocally negative. At best our words and concepts give us fragmentary and prejudiced clues as to the nature of things. Remembering our treatment of John Locke seems to magnify the problem, for we must not forget that the "things" our words describe are actually our experiences, which we presume to be connected to some objective world external to our own minds. Even these experiences themselves are often too rich to be captured exhaustively by linguistic symbols. So what are the chances that my experience is correlated accurately to a world outside my mind, that my vocabulary is adequate to give a precise and literal description of that experience, that the lines of communication between my mind and yours are free of static, that your vocabulary is similar enough to mine for you to attach the right meanings to the symbols I have conveyed, and finally, that your experiences are similar enough to mine that you can "catch my meaning"? It seems just short of miraculous that our words carry any meaning at all.

Yet the modern scientific mindset whose origins we have traced to Galileo and Descartes would have us believe that the set of symbols it employs are (at least potentially) accurate, unambiguous, and literally true. The kind of certainty sought by these and other scientifically-minded individuals would seem to require a one-to-one correspondence between these symbols and the things to which they refer. Does science presume that its symbols can be so correlated? One of the founders of modern logic, and one of the twentieth century's seminal thinkers believes that science often does, in fact, make this erroneous claim.

Whitehead and "Misplaced Concreteness"

Maybe during Descartes' time it was not unreasonable to expect that someday humans would achieve knowledge that is certain about important truths. In the time since that confident era philosophers have beat a substantial, if not steady, retreat from this quest. But dreams of certainty die hard, and many persons still cling to the hope of discovering incontrovertible proof of important claims about the universe.

Among other things, such proof would require a literal and unambiguous means of symbolizing those things about which one would speak. As related in chapter 1, much of philosophy in the early twentieth century was directed toward creating this symbolic apparatus that would be the vehicle for certainty. One key player in the attempt to formulate a purified language of logic was Alfred North Whitehead, the English mathematician and philosopher who settled in the United States in the 1920s. Later in his career he became one of the harshest critics of any claims of certainty that boasted a scientific basis.

The portions of Whitehead's thought relevant to our discussion surround his notion of "the fallacy of misplaced concreteness." As one would expect, this notion parallels a number of ideas of Henri Bergson. Both of these thinkers, unlike many persons still committed to a more Cartesian tradition, gave serious philosophical attention to the passage of time. In Western intellectual history, the awareness that things really change with the passing of time is a relatively recent phenomenon. The serious study of history has a very short history.

Whitehead, considered the father of process philosophy, shared with Bergson the conviction that the clarity and fixity of mathematical symbols and concepts were not reflected in nature. They believed that the symbolism of language was inadequate to the task of circumscribing any natural event that takes place in the flux and flow of the actual world. Concepts, ideas, equations, and the like exist in the rarefied and changeless propositional space of Plato. In this space everything is perfect. Everything is singular. Meaning and Being are the same. This "virtual" logical space is nonphysical, changeless, and clean. It is the world of Π, e, the Pythagorean theorem, and F=ma. The flow of time has no home here, since time introduces unpredictability, it is generative and destructive, and very messy. But the concepts and words we employ have, in fact, grown up exactly in this world of change. So the words, irreducibly historical in their origins, are stretched beyond their competency when made to house "eternal" truths. Then the mistakenly absolutized notions are turned back upon the changeable world that gave them birth, seeking to constrain arbitrarily a dynamic world in a static conceptual straitjacket. This is one way in which concreteness is misplaced.

As we try to articulate the form of this world of perfect ideas, Whitehead notes: "Weakness of insight and deficiencies of language stand in the way inexorably. Words and phrases must be stretched towards a generality foreign to their ordinary usage; and however such elements of language be stabilized as technicalities, they remain metaphors mutely appealing for an imaginative leap."[4] So logicians and mathematicians, philosophers and theologians, might have a very clear and wide agreement on the meaning of certain terms, but the referent of many of these terms remains a matter of controversy, if not mystery. Symbols such as "Π," "truth," or even "God" may have a relatively clear meaning, settled by convention among a certain group of persons where each symbol has become "stabilized as a technicality." (But has anyone ever actually, undoubtedly, clearly, and distinctly experienced a circle whose circumference stands precisely in the prescribed ratio to its diameter, or a statement whose clarity and referent are unarguable, or the ultimate source of all being?) We presume, perhaps by an imaginative leap of faith, that these words refer to something, but the distance between the word and any actual referent all but guarantees some imprecision in the fit.

Making a very similar point in a different way, Whitehead maintains:

> Philosophy has been haunted by the unfortunate notion that its method is dogmatically to indicate premises which are severally clear, distinct, and certain; and to erect upon those premises a deductive system of thought. But the accurate expression of the final generalities is the goal of discussion and not its origin. Philosophy has been misled by the example of mathematics; and even in mathematics the statement of the ultimate logical principles is beset with difficulties, as yet insuperable.[5]

The ostensibly purified language of mathematics, even while not as purely consistent and clear as it seemed, is deficient to capture a world of process. Even mathematical concepts have a history, and this history belies mathematics' attempt at timelessness. It is no wonder that contingent, historical realities continues to blur the boundaries of any mathematical construct that would seek to describe them. The world of mathematical concept, at least as traditionally seen (a world of Platonic essences), does not grow. At least practically no one until Charles Peirce spoke coherently of the development of such an ideal world.

Whitehead thought that science's attempt to superimpose that allegedly clean and well-defined world upon this messy one could never finally succeed. Equations cannot even perfectly describe actual bodies in motion or their changes through time. They are surely then not competent to provide a complete picture of the messy experiences of human beings such as love, death, hope, and childbirth. We must look beyond the

Platonic vocabulary of geometry and number if we are to frame a proper engagement with the spasmodic world of time and change. Whitehead is among those who have helped supply the West with a vocabulary more suited to the stormy world we all navigate. Later we will see how science is now contributing to his kind of vocabulary, as the scientific community more broadly affirms the end of certainty.

Plato and the Ancient Conversation

Descartes' dream of a world of mathematical certainty was not original. At least since Pythagoras, a good number of thinkers have shared the desire to live amid the purity and indubitability of mathematical objects. Western history's most influential thinker, Plato (427/8–347/8 BCE), was very much taken with this Pythagorean vision. In discussions about math, certainty, and the natural world, Plato is usually portrayed as the West's quintessential apologist for the priority of logic and concept. He was very distrustful of time and duration, preferring instead to expend his mental energies in search of the eternal and changeless. His well-known "realm of the Forms" is the repository for these eternal perfections.

Conceived by way of mathematical examples, this heavenly realm contains all of the perfect patterns of things whose imperfect counterparts we experience in the world of the physical. For example, we understand perfectly well what "flatness" is despite the complete absence of a physical example of it. So "flatness itself" must exist in some other place. Sometimes he called this other place "heaven." Likewise, we have a strong sense that "goodness," "justice," and "beauty" all refer to some actual quality, even though we never experience the pure version in this world. So these, and many other perfections, exist in the nonphysical, nonchanging, nontemporal, nondecaying heavenly realm. This realm can be approached by humans to the extent that they are able to free their souls (minds) from the chaotic world of matter. Since our souls ultimately share with the heavenly forms the qualities of changelessness and immateriality, souls, unlike bodies, have what it takes to transcend this notoriously ill-behaved material realm.

Though this two-realm theory of reality, where the ideal mathematized world is the preferred world, is rightly called "platonic," there is more to Plato's view than this simple affirmation of duality. He realized, for example, that there are serious faults in his own views, most notably surrounding the proper description of the relationship between the two realms. Further, though he was a mathematician, he was also something of a mystic, often describing with ecstatic poetic imagery his own kind of "beatific vision" of what heaven must look and feel like.[6] He recognized, at least incipiently, the same kinds of limitations of linguistic reference that are later reprised by Bergson, Nietzsche, Whitehead, and others. This recognition concerns us here.

The questions about the adequacy of symbols, whether mathematical or otherwise, to represent objects of experience is actually the same problem as the one about the relationship of the world of forms to the world of matter. In book five of *The Republic*, Plato relates the difficulty of ascribing any name unambiguously to any physical object (though "names" are much more than mere names for Plato).

> Will you be so very kind, sir, as to tell us whether, of all these beautiful things, there is one which will not be found ugly; or of the just, which will not be found unjust; or of the holy, which will not also be unholy?
>
> No, he replied; the beautiful will in some point of view be found ugly; and the same is true of the rest. And may not the many which are doubles be also halves?—doubles, that is, of one thing, and halves of another?
>
> Quite true.[7]

With these words Plato is attempting to show how the ever-changing world of our sense experience, the physical world, resists being captured cleanly by a concept. Because anything we describe one way might, under different circumstances, be described by opposite terms, he argued that our thinking is more profitably applied to the eternal realm. In that realm we encounter beauty, holiness, justice, and other realities in their pure form, not just in their relative exemplifications. In that world the meanings of our thoughts do not slip and slide between being and not-being; they reside in a kind of nonreferential purity of absolute Being. On earth, unlike in heaven, the objects of our concepts are never certain. Much of our deliberation begins to look like silly plays on words:

They are like the punning riddles which are asked at feasts or the children's puzzle about the eunuch aiming at the bat, with what he hit him, as they say in the puzzle, and upon what the bat was sitting. The individual objects of which I am speaking are also a riddle, and have a double sense: nor can you fix them in your mind, either as being or not-being, or both, or neither.[8]

The children's riddle to which Plato referred probably went something like this: "A man who was not a man saw and did not see a bird which not a bird sitting on a branch that was not a branch and hit and did not hit it with a stone that was not a stone." If objects of our contemplation have no more clarity (or reality) than that described here, then our claims to know anything at all are in deep trouble. The "solution" to the riddle is this: "a half-blind eunuch threw a pumice-stone at a bat perched on a reed, inflicting a glancing blow." Plato was convinced that our thinking processes could indeed accomplish more than this, and that our quest for truth was much more than clever word-games.

This conviction (among others) led him to propose a heaven from which these intellectual problems were banished. There must exist, in his system, an intelligible region where, as his philosophical forbear had said, "knowing and being are the same."[9] Since certainty seemed impossible in this world of appearances, we must seek it elsewhere. Since the corruptible world of the flesh always eluded our attempts at unambiguous reference, we might anachronistically attribute to Plato the contention that "flesh and blood shall not inherit the kingdom of heaven." (Of course, the thought patterns of Plato were in the background of much New Testament literature.) The soul, which shares with these heavenly perfections the attributes of unity and immateriality, is the part of us that is able to ascend into this spiritual plane, and only there may it "consort with reality."[10]

Many references to Plato and to "Platonism" end here, with his preference for the ultimate reality of those objects in the intelligible realm. We must not forget, however, that he was acutely aware of the problems with this view of things. Moreover, he never claimed to have a clear understanding of the final content of this heavenly realm. Salvation for Plato always retained a sharp sense of mystery. It seemed that this situation alternately inspired and irritated him. The mathematician in him resisted loose ends and unanswered questions. The mystic in him resisted easy answers. Socrates, whose recorded words are usually indistinguishable from those of Plato, his only recorder, finally concluded that he had gained a reputation for wisdom because the people presumed that he "possessed the wisdom that [he] found lacking in others."[11] In reality, Socrates understood that neither he nor his detractors knew anything truly good or beautiful. His only advantage was that at least he was aware of and inspired by the mystery.[12] And he dedicated his life to the passionate quest for and committed service to this ultimate unknown.

So, while Plato might seem the prime antagonist to any effort announcing the impossibility of certainty, his mystical inclinations might be invoked actually to bolster the argument. In many ways his contradictions are our own. Like the Pythagoreans, Plato was both mathematician and mystic. He was inspired by the prodigious power of number and geometry, but was cognizant of the inability of the formal world to be mapped exhaustively onto the world of experience. He never had a confident explanation of how the intelligible realm affected the sensible (available to the five senses) realm, yet he was sure of the connection. Albert Einstein was amazed at the same conundrum, as attested by his famous saying that "the eternal mystery of the world is its comprehensibility."[13] Einstein was, as we are still, asking Plato's question. It is no wonder that Alfred North Whitehead once described all of Western philosophy as a "series of footnotes to Plato."[14]

The Signs Are All Around Us
C. S. Peirce

Charles Sanders Peirce (1839–1914) was the most subtle and gifted American thinker of his time. He is still regarded by many as the most original philosopher that the United States has produced, though he is not (yet) the most famous. He will emerge as the primary hero of this book, as his ideas will serve as catalysts for developing a number of useful responses to contemporary issues between science and religion. Among the reasons for his relative obscurity in the earlier decades of this century is that he never published a book-length exposition of his ideas. What we know of his ideas has been gleaned from a rather chaotic set of papers published in a variety of periodicals over a period of more than forty years, some unpublished papers, and a number of letters. He also never held a permanent faculty position at any university; thus he was denied the platform from which most academic publications are launched.

Yet his influence on other thinkers was profound. Among the best-known persons clearly inspired by Peirce's philosophical insights were William James and John Dewey. These two seminal thinkers promoted many Peircean ideas and helped earn Peirce the title of "founder" of American pragmatism. For the purposes of this essay, Peirce will be cited in connection with chance, the future, theory of knowledge, scientific method, salvation, and faith. But first, let us examine his contributions to the questions of this chapter, about how we use language to refer to objects of our experience.

Peirce would have shared with Bergson, Nietzsche, Whitehead, and Plato the belief that our words are not adequate to capture a natural or concrete thing in an unambiguous fashion. We see Peirce foreshadowing a now very widespread movement known as "fuzzy logic" in this quote from the *Dictionary of Philosophy and Psychology*:

> Think of arm chairs and reading chairs and dining-room chairs, and kitchen chairs, chairs that pass into benches, chairs that cross the boundary and become settees, dentist's chairs, thrones, opera stalls, seats of all sorts, those miraculous fungoid growths that cumber the floor of the arts and crafts exhibitions, and you will see what a lax bundle in fact is this simple straightforward term. I would undertake to defeat any definition of chair or chairishness that you gave me.[15]

Thus there is no fixed referent for even this simple word. A similar analysis could be applied to any name of any category. Categories that change, even more obviously, resist a clean-cut definition. And what things do not change at least a little bit?

But so far our analysis has only been critical. We have discussed what words and concepts built upon them cannot do, with little attention to what they can do. Peirce has become known as the creator of an entire discipline aimed at exposing and explaining the function of words and ideas. This study, semiotics (or semeiotics, to use Peirce's preferred spelling), is the analysis of signs. Though what counts as a sign differs from one semiotic thinker to another, most agree that words are fundamentally signs.

(For Peirce, words are clearly not the only kinds of signs, but they are a crucial kind of sign and provide a good model for understanding what signs in general are.)

A famous passage from Peirce provides a good starting point for the discussion of his understanding of "sign." "A sign, or representamen, is something which stands to somebody for something in some respect or capacity."[16] So when Bill speaks a word to Ted, a sign is used to communicate an idea between them. This process is irreducibly triadic, involving (1) the "original" sign, (2) the object for which the sign stands for, and (3) the new sign initiated in the mind of the one who receives it (the interpretant). So when Bill speaks the word "pepper" to Ted, the word is not the object. The word stands for the object, and it stands for the object in some respect to Ted. An "interpretant," which is immediately a new sign, is then formed in the mind of Ted due to Bill's communication with him. Whether the sign formed in Ted's mind is about a seasoning, a type of baseball game, or the name of a family pet will depend on a number of factors related to Bill and Ted's contexts. Peirce discusses these contextual matters at great length, but they will not concern us here.

The relevant point now is the irreducible complexity and changeability of the signing process. Every sign, by virtue of its very existence as a sign, is triadic, meaning it always involves sign, object, and interpretant. There is simply no way around this structure. For Peirce, the sign

> addresses somebody, that is, creates in the mind of that person an equivalent sign, or perhaps a more developed sign. That sign which it creates I call the interpretant of the first sign. The sign stands for something, its object. It stands for that object, not in all respects, but in reference to a sort of idea, which I have sometimes called the ground of the representamen.[1]

Notice that the sign cannot stand for the object "in all respects," but only in reference to another idea or ideas. So when you hear a combination of words (or you see, hear, or feel anything at all), the object or event referred to in those words can never be isolated as an autonomous thing. Much like with Bergson and many other modern thinkers, the sign is not the thing and can pick out only some very limited characteristics of the object to which it refers, and those only in relation to other ideas. Complete and literal reference to any fixed thing seems quite impossible.

Moreover, this relational function of signs is the very essence of signs. Signs (including those that are words), therefore, exist only as they participate in this sort of relationship. If Peirce is right, Plato's hope that ultimately words might be tied to essences in some permanent identity is crushed by the very nature of words as signs. Even in private contemplation, when we might work closely with concepts we employ very consistently, the fact that our words have "grown up" irreducibly as signs renders this Platonic hope unachievable. For example, when I re-read my own words several weeks or months after first writing them, several just don't seem right anymore. As I learn and grow, the meanings of even key concepts and beliefs change.

Furthermore, it can be seen that the interpretant is immediately a new sign, and the triadic structure is repeated. Even if Ted is just thinking to himself, he is thinking in signs. This is because for as long as Ted is thinking "pepper," his mind is communicating a sign from himself to himself from moment to moment. His noon self delivers a sign to his 12:01 PM self, and the time lapse can be subdivided as finely as you like. Each moment of successive entertainment of a thought involves all the complex "triadicity" of signhood. This is because the noon self must communicate the sign to the noon-plus-one self, which sign moves from being interpretant at noon to being a new sign at noon-plus-one, but as soon as the sign is created at noon-plus-one it is the interpretant of noon's sign as delivered. So the sign never "settles down" into some formulaic existence. Each sign is "bottomless" in that we can never think a foundation for a sign that is not itself a sign.

All of this applies to signs other than words. Any experience of which we are aware requires this semeiotic structure. If I look out my window and see a hawk riding a breeze, the experience, as soon as I can even recognize it, is already a sign. As soon as it makes an impact on my consciousness, it does so as sign. For Peirce (and most postmoderns), the sign is always already interpreted, whether it is a visible image, a twinge of arthritis pain, a sudden memory of yesterday's events, or a written or spoken word. If things happen to us uninterpreted, then we are not aware of them (in this latter particular, Peirce echoes Kant).

So what happens to our attempts at capturing some object or event in the unrelenting jaws of certainty? Well, according to Peirce and the others cited in this chapter, our words are not up to the task. Many philosophers, Plato among them, lamented this element of the human condition and sought release from the vagaries of sign-thinking. The analytic philosophers largely sought for an unambiguous language of referring that would dissolve those irritating quandaries of the philosophers, which the analysts saw as results of linguistic ambiguities. Bergson, Whitehead, and Peirce, (and maybe Nietzsche, who really belongs in a category all his own) argued, though in different ways, that language's attempts to describe exhaustively and literally a reality beyond signs was, in fact, a foray into regions unsuited to the true purposes of words. With the inability of words to circumscribe even the simplest features of our experiences, hopes of certainty seem dashed.

Dictionaries in Heaven?

Maybe a rather absurd image will serve to illustrate much contemporary thought about the state of the West's "Platonic" quest for certainty. Many contemporary thinkers are more apt to think that what Plato referred to as a realm of eternal and changeless forms is really rather a realm of an evolving dictionary. Where Plato thought that true intellectual dialogue was about an immaterial world of essences and truth, at best only hinted at by our pedestrian attempts at rational discourse, most today see this discourse as being about signs of some kind or another. For example, where do we go to find out what Beauty really is? For Plato, one must make the arduous upward journey toward intellectual and spiritual purification, one day emerging into the light of Beauty itself. For most of us today, we start with the dictionary. I am being only about half flippant here, for the meanings of our words can theoretically be described very well by a dictionary.

The problem with dictionary definitions, though, is that they are made up of words. And these words, if they are to be understood, must also be looked up in the dictionary. And their definitions, too, will be made up of words. Eventually you end up where you started, wondering what Beauty really is. Is there ever any way to get beyond the circular process of defining words with other words and to land with our feet planted on some *terra firma* of assured knowledge? Can our reasoning processes ever do any more than play clever games whose rules are set out by the meanings assigned in a dictionary, a book whose definitions are arrived at by convention, rather than by eternal necessity? Does the modern view of concepts as signs tied to other signs leave us awash in a dizzying downpour of pure arbitrariness? Is there not some connection between this dictionary-land and our experience? How exactly does the world of concepts fit onto the world of living and dying? In essence, these questions are confronting along with Einstein the mystery of the world's comprehensibility. We must admit that dictionary definitions are at best a starting place for a serious quest for meanings; they are not the end.

A view of the world that takes faith and science seriously and contains a good dose of Peircean semeiotics may well provide a response to this mystery that does not leave the seeker lost in a hopeless fog. At the very least, a worldview that avoids the abyss of meaninglessness will have to reshape existing questions and expose the surreptitious assumptions of the certainty-seeking modern world. For this response to take shape, however, the futility of the quest of the certainty seeker must first be drawn in sharper relief. No conversation does this better than one addressing chance and randomness.

Notes

[1] *Introduction to Metaphysics*, T. E. Hulme, trans. (New York: G. P. Putnam's Sons, 1912) 17-18.

[2] Quoted in E. H. Gombrich, *Art and Illusion: A Study in the Psychology of Pictorial Representation*. (Princeton NJ: Princeton University Press, 1960) 86.

[3] Ibid., 87.

[4] *Process and Reality*, corrected ed., David Ray Griffin and Donald W. Sherburne, eds. (New York: Free Press., 1978) 4.

[5] Ibid., 8.

[6] *The Republic*, 490a-b.

[7] Ibid., 479a-b.

[8] Ibid., 479c.

[9] Quoted in John Mansley Robinson, *An Introduction to Early Greek Philosophy* (Boston: Houghton-Mifflin Co., 1968) 110.

[10] *The Republic*, 490a-b.

[11] Plato, *Apology*, 23a

[12]Ibid.

[13]*Out of My Later Years* (New York: Philosophical Library, 1950) 61.

[14]Quoted in Forrest Baird and Walter Kaufmann, eds., *Ancient Philosophy*, 2d ed. (Upper Saddle River NJ: Prentice-Hall, 1997) 66.

[15]*Dictionary of Psychology and Philosophy*, 1902. Quoted in Bart Kosko, *Fuzzy Thinking: The New Science of Fuzzy Logic.* (New York: Hyperion, 1993) 121. Kosko's book is an excellent introduction to logic's own movement away from the hopes of certainty.

[16]CP 2:228. References to Peirce will normally utilize standard procedure in citing volume and paragraph number from *The Collected Papers of Charles Sanders Peirce*, Charles Hartshorne and Paul Weiss, eds. (Cambridge MA: Harvard University Press, 1937).

[17]Ibid. The meaning of "ground" in this context is controversial and will not be addressed here. For further treatment of this notion and a brief introduction to the philosophy of Peirce, see John K. Sheriff *Charles Peirce's Guess at the Riddle. Grounds for Human Significance.* (Bloomington IN: Indiana University Press, 1994).

For Further Reading

Hausman, Carl. *Charles S. Peirce's Evolutionary Philosophy.* Cambridge: Cambridge University Press, 1993.

Kaufmann, Walter. *Nietzsche: Philosopher, Psychologist, Antichrist.* 4th ed. Princeton NJ: Princeton University Press, 1974.

Lakoff, George, and Mark Johnson. *Metaphors We Live By.* Chicago: University of Chicago Press, 1980.

Percy, Walker. *Lost in the Cosmos: The Last Self-Help Book.* New York: Farrar, Straus, & Giroux, 1983.

Sheriff, John K. *Charles Peirce's Guess at the Riddle: Grounds for Human Significance.* Bloomington IN: Indiana University Press, 1994.

Chapter 3

Real Randomness?

In the movie *Back to the Future* the main character confronts his contingency when he discovers that his time-travel exploits have resulted in his preventing his mother and father from ever meeting. If he is unable to return to the past and get his folks back together again, he will fade from existence. Most of us ponder the reasons behind our existence. Did my parents meet by chance? What if they had not met at all? What if they had conceived a child the month before I was conceived? Could I be the result of chance, a radically contingent being whose chances of existing at all were minuscule at best?

This chain of contingency can be traced further back into history, of course, and quickly we realize that even apparently trivial minutiae, had they differed even a little, would have prevented any one of us, or all of us, from existing at all. It may even be that some of these events, though they ended up being crucial for our very being, happened purely by chance. Such a scenario is at least suggested by evolutionary theory as understood by Darwin and his followers. Our dissatisfaction at this suggestion is understandable, especially if we, like most persons with religious convictions, believe that universal history has some kind of purpose. But a real role for chance is being affirmed by more and more persons, both within the sciences and elsewhere. Later we will see how chance and plan are not really antagonists at all and may in fact be necessary partners in any drama involving actual persons.

Random Inclinations

What role did chance events play in the origin of human beings and in the origin of the universe? Some of the most contentious interchanges between people of faith and people of science have been sparked by attempted answers to this question. For some people, the idea that random processes occur at all is anathema. For others, such processes do not appear threatening at all. Much of the debate between pro-chance and anti-chance advocates is due to misunderstandings about the meaning of the word "chance." However, much of the debate is also traceable to profoundly conflicting inclinations of human minds. One of the most fascinating ongoing debates of the twentieth century took place between two of its most renowned physicists, Niels Bohr and Albert Einstein. Bohr was convinced, due to revolutionary discoveries in microscopic physics, that subatomic reality sometimes behaved in ways that could not be explained. Einstein was repulsed by this notion, ridiculing the idea by suggesting that "God does not play dice" with the universe. Most influential thinkers in the history of the Western world have affirmed Einstein's perspective, but many contemporary debates about chance and law, though instigated by peculiarly modern circumstances, have revealing parallels in ancient times.

The ancient Greek philosopher Epicurus died in about 271 BCE. The great American philosopher Charles Sanders Peirce died in 1914. In the 2,100-plus years that separate the writings of these two outstanding thinkers, practically no one thought that chance, or randomness, played a fundamental role in nature. No one thought that any events should be explained by the notion of random events as causes. Since Peirce, however, that has changed dramatically. Today, philosophers and scientists by the thousands are suggesting that plenty of things might happen just for that reason—no reason at all. This suggestion is offensive to our rational sensibilities, which seek full explanations of all things and thus presume that these explanations are there to be found.

The rise of the sciences of chance, from statistical mechanics to quantum mechanics and, more recently, to chaos theory, has caused the role of chance to be taken very seriously. The notion of chance is extremely subtle and subject to easy misinterpretation. Properly conceived, however, many concepts surrounding the idea of chance can contribute considerably to our understanding of the world. These ideas can help us see quite clearly why even many scientists today are finding the end of certainty.

The concept of chance is one of the most frightening, fruitful, and confusing ideas of the modern period. It is frightening because it has the potential to challenge our conviction that things can be explained. Nevertheless, it has been enormously fruitful for contemporary physics, even to the point where physics today is unimaginable without it. Yet most of the people who use the notion do so without any clear sense of what they mean by it. Since the role of chance, or randomness, is one of the major elements of the end of certainty in the twentieth century, it is imperative that we explore some of the fascinating history of the idea, so that we might develop a clearer understanding of its meaning and its proper place in our universe of explanations. Let us begin with an ancient Greek genius.

Great Moments in the History of Chance I
Epicurus

Democritus (fifth and fourth centuries BCE) was one of the earliest persons to suggest that the basic components of the universe were invisibly tiny particles called "atoms." This contemporary of Socrates had a great influence on successive generations of thinkers, and this influence was nowhere more evident than in the teachings of Epicurus (342–271 BCE) and his followers, the Epicureans. Epicurus based his vastly influential philosophical system on the atomism of Democritus. But Epicurus came to espouse a version of atomism that Democritus surely would have rejected, for Democritus apparently believed (along with his teacher Leucippus) that the only realities were "atoms and the void," and that "everything happens by reason and by necessity."[1] Epicurus, too, believed that the only ultimately real things were atoms and the void, but he denied that everything must happen by reason and necessity.

For Epicurus, atoms might "swerve" for no reason at all. This swerve is called the *clinamen*, from the Greek for "turn, change, lean." We get our English word "recline" from the same root. Just as we move from a straight, vertical position in order to recline, Epicurus' atoms sometimes deviate from their expected straight, vertical motion. In his view, primordial times saw the parallel downward movement of an infinite number of tiny, indivisible atoms (Greek *a-tom*, "not divisible"). If only necessity governed their motions, then no two atoms ever could have collided. Hence no two atoms ever could have joined together or bounced off one another. Then the world of composite, divisible objects we see today could never have formed. Since it is obvious even to the untutored that things stick together and fly apart, something must have happened to have begun the process of unification and dispersal that we see all around us. If lawlike progression of movement were the only possibility, as Democritus claimed, then the atoms would still be falling in parallel lines.

In some cases the atoms swerved. Some small number veered off of their previous course without influence from any collision with a neighbor. So the only "explanation" for this first collision is chance. The atom, or atoms, just swerved. Why did they swerve? There is no reason why they swerved; they just did. And once at least one of the atoms swerved, the entire population of atoms was forever disrupted. Very quickly a chaos of collisions ensues. Some atoms, presumably because of their shape, stuck together. Other atoms, shaped in such a way as to discourage union, rebounded off of each other. After many eons of such collisions, the vastly varied world we live in took shape. This world usually behaves in an orderly fashion, but we must also realize that there is still some percentage of atoms prone to the *clinamen*, and hence the world remains an unpredictable place. It is a world where human actions are not necessarily dictated by the configurations of the smallest components of matter. In other words, there are events, which may include human choices and actions, that are not the predetermined outcomes of atomic motions.

Epicureanism thus differed considerably from the other main philosophical school of the Hellenistic period, Stoicism. Though both systems of thought taught that people should seek inner peace, they held to diametrically opposite positions with regard to the chance question. The Stoics, for whom all things were part of a rational deity, believed that nothing ever happened that was not eternally predestined to happen, and thus that humans can have no effect on the events of the universe. Everything has a reason rooted in God's own nature, so it was foolish to resist or to be disturbed by any event. If God's infinite wisdom has ordained it, then it must happen, and we cannot change it. Hence we should be no more anxious about the death of a child than we are about the breaking of a clay pot. Pots break, people die, and since God's infinite rationality has so determined the cosmos, we should react without feeling. If we truly comprehend that all things happen as they must, then nothing will ever disturb us, and we will have achieved the desired state of complete inner peace.

Now clearly not many persons in Western history have actually sought the Stoic goal of apathy as the main aim of their lives, and far fewer have accomplished it. But, in one of the perennial paradoxes of that history, most people have adopted a worldview that has much in common with stoicism. At a very general level most have believed that everything does in fact happen for a reason, though there is wide disagreement as to the nature of those reasons. Philosophical thought throughout Western history, at least since the ebb of Epicurean influence, has been about which reasons are correct, presuming that explanations of the desired type are there to be found. The idea that some events may not have specific explanations of desired types was not given serious philosophical attention again until the nineteenth century.

Chance and Explanation

Before exploring Charles Peirce's contribution to the debates about chance, a bit of clarification is necessary. What exactly is meant by the assertion that some event happens "by chance?" What is the positive content of the claim that an atom swerves "at random?" We will see shortly that neither of these questions can be answered as asked. This is because any claim of chance, or better, randomness, is fundamentally a negative claim.

To claim that an event happens at random is to admit the absence of an explanation of some type. This absence might be due to limitations on human observational power, or it might be fundamental. Therefore, claims of randomness may also assert that the desired explanation is not only unavailable, but nonexistent. In either case the assertion of chance is one of ignorance about an explanation of the event in question. What many expositors miss in their treatments of chance or randomness is the realization that there are many different kinds of explanations. When an event is said to be a random occurrence, usually a specific kind of explanation is claimed to be absent. Such an assertion says nothing about the potential availability of other kinds of explanations. So there are potentially as many kinds of randomness as there are explanations. These points can be illustrated easily.

A perfectly alert and healthy young man is driving his sportscar through a narrow mountain pass on a rainy day. Just as he rounds one of many blind curves on this frequently traveled road, a boulder, loosened by the rain's erosion of the soil, falls onto his car, resulting in fatal injuries to the driver. Naturally, his shocked and grieved family and friends seek an explanation for this tragedy. The highway engineers also want an explanation. So does his life insurance company. The three groups of seekers are looking for at least three different kinds of explanations. The family seeks to come to grips with great loss and pain and may look to God for reassurance that his death was not meaningless. The highway engineers look carefully for the conditions and causes that led to the accident. The insurance company wishes to certify that this was indeed an accident, knowing that a certain percentage of men his age die every year. Presumably, other persons would search for even different types of explanations.

For brevity's sake we might name the three types of explanations mentioned above as intentional, causal-physical, and statistical (the last not even qualifying as an explanation of the single event). This list is neither exhaustive, nor are the items mutually exclusive. Each asks, "Why did he die?" but looks for a different kind of answer. The family wants to know if God had some reason for the man's death at this time, thus desiring an explanation containing an intentional choice by a personal agent. The engineers wish to prevent further incidents of this type and wish to know the physical conditions of the soil and stones. Thus they will measure the density of the soil, the stability of the rocks, the amount of rainfall, and other quantifiable data. The insurance company might want to confirm that this was not a suicide (thus precluding the presence of an intentional explanation), and then would "explain" the man's death by suggesting that the event falls within statistical expectations. Note that this last analysis is not an explanation of the single tragedy at all, but an admission of the absence of certain kinds of explanations, ones that would remove the event from the relevant statistical category (accident).

At various points in the attempts to explain this death, one might hold that the event was random in some sense. Those who would invoke randomness would usually do so in connection with the first type of explanation, the intentional. If the wreck is called a "freak accident," this is meant, among other things, to indicate that it was improbable, probably unavoidable, and definitely unintended. To say that it was random in this sense is to assert that it was not part of someone's plan for this rock to come loose precisely at the moment when the car rounded the curve. It is random because there is no intentional explanation for it.

On the other hand, the engineers are not likely to consider that their kind of explanation is absent. They wish to find a precise, quantifiable description of the circumstances of the accident, in order to predict when such things will occur in the future. They want to be able to say that "whenever X amount of rain falls on Y soil, rock, and slope conditions, then the embankment will become unstable." A claim of randomness in this effort is at least unhelpful, and very likely dangerous, as it would amount to the abandonment of the attempt to alleviate future dangerous conditions. Many would also say that there is no room for randomness in physical explanations, believing it incoherent to suppose that any physical event can happen without some physical cause. Still, those of an Epicurean disposition might indeed suggest that at some microscopic level a *clinamen* might have been the decisive motion that triggered the fall at that particular moment. Fortunately for our technological age, most engineers are not Epicureans.

There is a sense in which the insurance company conceives of the event precisely as random. Relatively stable numbers of men in certain age groups are killed in automobile accidents each year. Insurance companies know this, and adjust their rates accordingly. They don't know, of course, whether a given individual will die in a wreck or not. In just the same manner, the casino owner does not know who will win the next hand of blackjack, but he does know, with great precision, how much revenue can be expected from his blackjack enterprises for the month. Each hand is treated as a random variable, an accidental, unpredictable event. "Accident," as used in the classical philosophical sense, denotes an event or quality that does not "have to be." Does this mean that there are events that are completely "uncaused," that fall outside our "causal pattern" explanations, but are governed by higher level statistical patterns? Is it possible for wholes to be predicted even if their parts cannot?

Great Moments in the History of Chance II
Charles Sanders Peirce

America's greatest philosopher earned his living for most of his life in areas outside the practice of philosophy. He worked for over thirty years as a research scientist for the U. S. Coast and Geodetic Survey, supervising and conducting a number of earth science experiments. He also worked occasionally for the Harvard Observatory. Such scientific employment was natural to a man who had graduated *summa cum laude* from Harvard's prestigious Lawrence Scientific School. Peirce was the first American scientist to represent his country at an international scientific association meeting.[2] The son of prominent Harvard mathematician Benjamin Peirce, Charles lived his entire life in the atmosphere and ethos of quantitative physical science. From photometrics to gravimetrics, Peirce was an internationally recognized scientific mind. Therefore it may appear surprising that he would be the one to break the two thousand year-old philosophical moratorium against questioning the lawlike behavior of the natural world. Perhaps even more surprising is that chance's premier modern advocate was also a master logician.

Though scientists by the thousands would come to affirm the role of chance and to question the very efficacy of natural causation itself within a few decades of Peirce's death, his prescient ideas in this area were revolutionary in the-turn-of-the-century intellectual climate. One might say that he heralded the arrival of real chance, but it is hard to call someone a herald if practically no one paid serious attention to the call. A number of different influences drove Peirce toward his insistence that randomness be taken seriously in scientific, philosophical, and logical discussions. Among those influences was his awareness of the earth's incredible biological diversity, his failure to see convincing evidence of thorough mechanism in Newtonian physics, and his conviction that humans exercise free will. A look at these three motivations will show how his conclusions about chance are actually natural outcomes of his life as a careful scientist. It was precisely his commitment to science and to its particular kind of thinking processes that would bring him to attack one of its most pervasive modern era convictions, that all nature operates according to strict and necessary laws.

Why Suppose Necessity?

Peirce notices that arguments for the universality of necessary causation are practically nonexistent. Most often, he contends, the doctrine of necessity is merely presumed, not demonstrated. In many circles a thinker is given a hearing only if he or she presumes a complete natural necessity. In Peirce's own words:

> When I have asked thinking men what reason they had to believe that every fact in the universe is precisely determined by law, the first answer has usually been that the proposition is a "presupposition" or postulate of scientific reasoning. Well, if that is the best that can be said for it, the belief is doomed. Suppose it be "postulated": that does not make it true, nor so much as afford the slightest rational motive for yielding it any credence. It is as if a man should come to borrow money and, when asked for his security, should reply he "postulated" the loan. To "postulate" a proposition is no more than to hope it is true.[3]

Peirce wonders about the reasons that might persuade a contemporary scientist toward necessitarianism. Expressing an idea that would not gain a significant following for another twenty-five years or so, Peirce offers that "there is room for serious doubt whether the fundamental laws of mechanics hold good for single atoms, and it seems quite likely that they are capable of motion in more than three dimensions."[4] One of the sources for this view was his Harvard training in chemistry, a study in which he found no reason to conclude the operation of complete mechanical necessity. In speculating on what might cause someone to believe in absolute law, Peirce concludes that he is uncertain, but that he knows one thing: "they cannot be real students of physical science—they cannot be chemists, for example."[5]

While the expectation that some sort of explanation exists for all possible phenomena is clearly reasonable, the presumption that a physical, causal explanation exists for each phenomenon may be unwarranted. But those who defend a natural necessity seem to equate "explanation" and "physical causal explanation." We have already seen that there are a number of different types of explanations for any given event, and Peirce argues that proponents of necessity are illegitimately requiring that one particular type of explanation be available for all events. However, just as not all events admit of an intentional explanation, Peirce contends that not all types of events have a mechanical-causal explanation.

He does not, of course, suggest that the affirmations of causal determinism are simply invented out of thin air. He cites Democritus as probably the first person to make a case for universal determinism. But Democritus, Peirce says, came to this conclusion because he limited his observations to only a small fraction of possible phenomena. Of this ancient determinism, Peirce relates:

> Its first advocate appears to have been Democritus, the atomist, who was led to it, as we are informed, by reflecting upon the "impenetrability, translation, and impact of matter . . ." That is to say, having restricted his attention to a field where no influence other than mechanical constraint could possibly come before his notice, he straightway jumped to the conclusion that throughout the universe that was the sole principle of action—a style of reasoning so usual in our day with men not unreflecting as to be more than excusable in the infancy of thought.[6]

If the model for one thing affecting another is rocks colliding, then there seems to be little room for more subtle effects. Or, to use a favorite English analogy from the eighteenth century, if all explanation relies on the model of colliding billiard-ball-like atoms, then a case for determinism seems evident. One must ask first, however, whether there is reason to believe that this model of causation is all-inclusive, or if it is superior to other models.

Not Necessarily Free

The overwhelming sense that humans choose freely is the oldest and most obvious challenge to the notion that the world operates according to a closed mathematical mechanism. Epicurus believed that natural determinism and free will were incompatible and opted for the *clinamen* as a refutation of the complete lawlikeness of nature. The Stoics shared this notion of incompatibility and chose to believe that free will was an illusion. Peirce sided with the Epicureans in this debate and believed that determinists who argue against the reality of free will are being at least disingenuous. He argues, using the term "necessitarian" to denote the one who insists that all the universe operates by lawful cause and effect, that:

I should not wonder if somebody were to suggest that perhaps the idea of a law is essential to the idea of one thing acting upon another. But surely that would be the most untenable suggestion in the world considering that there is no one of us who after lifelong discipline in looking at things from the necessitarian point of view has ever been able to train himself to dismiss the idea that he can perform any specifiable act of the will. It is one of the most singular instances of how a preconceived theory will blind a man to facts that many necessitarians seem to think that nobody really believes in the freedom of the will, the fact being that he himself believes in it when he is not theorizing.[7]

The argument from free will against natural law determinism, while not conclusive, is compelling to many persons. Peirce himself does not seem to believe that this case is conclusive, but he finds it at least interesting that even the most stringent advocates of necessitarianism still operate under the assumption that they can "perform any specifiable act of the will." If the world were governed by strict causal necessity, then my "decision" whether or not to have milk in my tea is necessitated by the laws of nature in conjunction with the antecedent conditions. There is no "freedom" to do without the milk this time, no freedom to skip teatime all together, no room in nature to do anything other than what the laws require.

These reflections do not prove that the necessitarian is wrong since our sense of being free to choose may be illusory. The main force of Peirce's case here is against the prevailing scientific tendency to presume an absolute causal necessity in the universe, and then to decide that free will is an illusion. This worldview precludes the consideration of evidence drawn from human experience. For Peirce, this approach is bad science, since it decides beforehand which kinds of evidence will count. Some of our experiences seem to show us a mechanical, law-driven cosmos. Others of our experiences seem to show us a universe with a future that is open and whose shape will be partially caused by the non-necessitated choices of human agents. In Peirce's words:

For, from the positions and velocities of the particles at any one instant, and the knowledge of the immutable forces, the positions at all other times are calculable; so that the universe of space, time, and matter is a rounded system uninterfered with from elsewhere. But, from the state of

47

feeling at any instant, there is no reason to suppose the states of feeling at all other instants are thus exactly calculable; so that feeling is, as I said, a mere fragmentary and illusive aspect of the universe. This is the way, then, that necessitarianism has to make up its accounts. It enters consciousness under the head of sundries, as a forgotten trifle; its scheme of the universe would be more satisfactory if this little fact could be dropped out of sight.[8]

Though the feeling of free choice may be the result of illusion, the experience of consciousness does not support such a conclusion. It is not fair of the necessitarians to rule the evidence of consciousness out of court without a hearing, allowing only evidence from things that behave like rocks.

Trial, Error, and Biodiversity

The incredible diversity of life on earth does not support the inference of a strict mechanical necessity in nature. Like so many observers, Peirce was moved and amazed at the way in which seemingly countless different kinds of life forms seem to inhabit practically every square inch of livable space on the earth. Peirce was struck by the phenomenon of biodiversity before there was even such a word. He was also very much persuaded of the Darwinian interpretation of life's history. Darwin's assertion that chance played a key role in evolution seemed just right to Peirce. Moreover, Peirce did not think a theory of mechanical necessity could account for such a prodigious variety of creatures, since their emergence required a real history with real growth.

Peirce asks himself if there has been an increase in variety since the time of the original nebula out of which our solar system formed and then answers the question thus:

It would seem as if there were an increase in variety, would it not? And yet mechanical law, which the scientific infallibilist tells us is the only agency of nature, mechanical law can never produce diversification.[9]

Darwin and his followers knew that the "laws" of heredity are statistical; that, for example, a certain percentage of children born to brown-eyed parents will have blue eyes. We cannot tell beforehand in detail the traits to be inherited by the children, so we retreat to a statistical level of prediction. Offspring will be shorter, taller, heavier, lighter, faster, slower, etc. than their parents. They will vary in hundreds of ways from their parents, and unpredictably so. Through this random variation of traits from generation to generation, a multitude of different forms has filled the earth. Peirce also knew that statistical descriptions had become indispensable in chemistry and physics, presumably the levels of description that apply to the component parts of the processes of biological inheritance. Variations analogous to those evident in biological history seemed to happen even in the chemistry lab. So if spontaneous or random variations drive heredity and if analogous variability happens even at microscopic scales (presumably among the molecules of heredity), at what point down the reductionist ladder should such variations be abandoned? According to Peirce, they should not be abandoned, and the only reason we would do so was if we were already committed to a necessitarian worldview. If, after Democritus, our models of all physical processes are pictures of rocks rolling down hills, then we might seek an explanation for hereditary variation that was mechanical and necessary. But since there is not sufficient reason to favor this model, a model that affirms real chance and real growth seems preferable.

Darwinian evolution, unlike some of the competing views of evolution, such as those of Lamarck or Spencer, affirmed the role of chance as the source of novel forms upon which natural selection could act. In Darwin's view, chance variations accumulating from one generation to the next eventually produce organisms better suited to survive in a given environment. Darwin himself did not address the rather philosophical question as to whether these chance variations were objectively, or inherently, random. His primary concern was not to speculate on whether or not there was a *clinamen* somewhere amid the microscopic genetic structure of an organism. Peirce was very interested in this kind of speculation. This is because he was seeking to develop a comprehensive metaphysic, a picture of the world that was consistent across all times and places and all scales of observation. He sought the best explanation for the big picture with a minimum of gaps and inconsistencies. He was convinced that his chancy worldview, which he called "tychism," was much better suited to account for a wider variety of observations than was its more popular rival, mechanical necessity.

Like the argument from freedom, this case is usually thought to be less than compelling because there is nothing in Darwinism that requires inherent chance. There are many ways in which deterministic processes might supply a very large amount of variations in genetic material. But also like the argument from freedom, the enormous diversification that has occurred as life has covered the earth does not support the inference of mechanical necessity. An unbiased survey of earth's biodiversity would not suggest the analogy of a machine, but rather a marvelous and pervasive example of the effectiveness of trial and error, with the successful trials accruing in certain hereditary lines, creating a kind of natural "habit" of perpetuating the successful forms. While it is true that neither our impression of freedom of the will nor Darwinian evolution is inconsistent with a universe of strict causal necessity, Peirce believes that these phenomena place the burden of proof upon the one who would advocate such a necessity. Evidence from biodiversity and freedom might certainly be explained away if there were overwhelming reasons to accept the strict and necessary causation favored by most natural scientists in the two centuries following Newton. For Peirce, these reasons simply do not exist, and though necessitarianism can never be decisively disproved, reasons for favoring it over tychism are woefully scarce.

For Peirce, when one examines the evolutionary history of life on earth, or the behavior of human beings, or even results of chemical reactions, factors other than mechanical causation appear to be at work. In none of these arenas do analogies of rocks or billiard balls appear to be the best. In both arenas events occur that seem to happen for reasons outside those explainable by mechanical causation. But doesn't natural science tell us that there is great benefit in applying the mechanical model to precisely those areas where it might not seem relevant? Clearly science has made great strides by preferring an automatic (or necessary, mechanical) model rather than one that invokes spirits, invisible forces, or gods and goddesses. Peirce is quite ready to admit as much, but he did not think that mechanical regularity was the last word for science. For him, denying mechanism was not the same as denying rationality, though many did and still do disagree with that assessment. To deny necessity is not to deny regularity. Peirce, like any decent scientist, was aware of the incredible degree to which the universe exhibited regularity. But he was not convinced that all of those deviations of experiment and observation from expected values could be attributed to errors of the experimenter or mechanical influences from unknown sources. Maybe some of nature's deviations from expected outcomes are due to the fact that the causal regularity of the cosmos is not complete. So Peirce revived the notion of the *clinamen* and suggested that there likely were infinitesimal deviations from mechanical regularity that occurred indefinitely often and larger deviations indefinitely infrequently. This "tychistic" understanding of the universe accounts better for a wider range of experience than does the mechanical view, especially now that natural scientists are more and more ready to affirm a substantial role for chance events.

Physical Science Vindicates Peirce

Charles Peirce was very much aware that some of the sciences admitted a role for randomness at some level. But most scientists presumed that the admission of chance was only a concession to human ignorance. If the full chemistry and physics of natural processes were known, then the complete lawfulness of nature would be evident, according to most natural scientists of his day. Peirce challenged this view by pointing to the human experience of freedom and of the apparent randomness in evolution that leads to novelty. But he suggested and argued more. He concluded that not even a chemist should infer necessity from observations of chemical reactions. And he questioned whether or not mechanical causation even applied in the micro-world of single atoms. Spontaneity, chance, or randomness, he conjectured, would show up even in the investigations of the "hard" sciences. This pronouncement proved prophetic.

Another inspiration for Peirce's advocacy of chance (other than his own training in math, logic, and chemistry) was the explosion of the statistical sciences in the one hundred or so years prior to his own work. Analysis of human populations had become an advanced mathematical science by Peirce's time. Analysts had documented the tremendous degree of statistical stability in birth, death, illness, and crime rates, for example. All of these humans, apparently acting independently and freely, behaved with an astounding collective regularity from year to year and generation to generation. As these "social scientists" developed more and more accurate mathematical tools for exposing and predicting trends in human behavior, natural scientists were applying similar tools to explain the collective behavior of physical particles whose tiny size made them individually inaccessible to observation. So according to the equations of Maxwell, for example, the collective behavior of billions and billions of atoms in an enclosed area would obey statistical laws with a great degree of regularity. We cannot know (either in the eighteenth century or now) what an individual human will do, but we can predict pretty well the percentage of thirty-five-year-olds that will die within the year. And we cannot know what an individual atom will do, but we can with confidence predict the rate at which heat will flow from the collective and interpret this result as the loss of kinetic energy of each of the particles comprising the collective.

These kinds of advances in statistical sciences were widely known and hailed during the nineteenth century. From these successes Peirce took a clue for his total view of the universe, for a comprehensive metaphysic. This was the step that most scientists were unwilling to make. The random motion of molecules of gas in a container was only random from our point of view, according to most physical scientists in Peirce's day. The unpredictable behavior of the individual human was only unpredictable from the limited human perspective. Natural science still presumed that there were laws that governed these entities but that our investigative and computational abilities were not sufficient to the task of illuminating the details. Peirce suggested that even full knowledge of the microscopic details would still not yield the desired explanatory or predictive results. Maybe people and atoms behave in ways that *can never* be accounted for mechanically. And maybe even microscopic deviations from complete uniformity will be seen to have momentous consequences in natural and human history.

Natural science in the decades since Peirce has powerfully vindicated his positions regarding the operation of chance. The hallmark of quantum physics in the twentieth century is the indeterminism of individual subatomic particles. As will be seen in part two of this book, conclusions drawn by such scientific luminaries as Max Planck, Niels Bohr, and Werner Heisenberg will underscore the inherent unpredictability (and hence incomplete explainability) of the micro-world. And chaos dynamics will highlight the possibility that microscopic and unpredictable events influence visible and crucial elements in nature. The statistical methods used by analysts of human populations and thermodynamically active fluids will come to be seen as essential even in subatomic physics. Admitting chance to the table hastened the end of certainty, in part because it helped introduce a sense of history into the analysis of what were thought to be systems running according to the "ahistorical" equations of physics. If chance is real, then the future is very different from the past.

Reductionism and the Arrow of Time

Much of the success of science in the modern era is owed to its reliance on reductionism, which, generally speaking, is the explanation of collective and complex systems or behaviors in terms of their simpler and smaller component parts. Reductionistic explanations help us understand a broader array of entities than more specialized descriptions of complex collectives. There are far fewer kinds of atoms than there are kinds of molecules, and, since all molecules are composed of atoms, our understanding of the behavior of these few kinds of atoms can help us understand the behavior of many different kinds of molecules. Analogously, there are many different kinds of human beings, but far fewer kinds of human organs. Our understanding of the human organism is greatly enhanced, then, by learning as much as possible about the component parts, since each kind of part follows its own set of rules that, in theory, are much less complex than the principles that guide the organism of which the organ is a part.

Radical reductionists, such as Francis Crick, co-discoverer of the structure of the DNA molecule, emboldened by the explanatory and predictive successes of delving deeply into the microscopic, believe that ultimately every complex entity can be understood by learning the rules that govern its simplest parts. On this view all of science can theoretically be "reduced" to physics, the study of the fundamental properties of matter. The macroscopic, or visible and measurable, properties of the gas could be explained and predicted with any desired degree of accuracy by knowing the details of the microscopic properties. If Peirce is right, and the motions of microscopic particles are at some level really random, then this form of radical reductionism will be in trouble because even full knowledge of the present complexion of atoms will not yield precise knowledge of future states. Thus does the presence of real randomness introduce into physics what many thinkers have called "the arrow of time."

The arrow of time points out the asymmetry of past and future, even in relatively simple systems such as a container of gas or a cup of tea. Past and future are different because the past is concrete and actual while the future is not. The presence of random events within a system guarantees that the future of that system is not written into its governing equations because inherently or absolutely unpredictable things might happen to such a system, creating a need to "reset" the values in the equations to account for the new situation.

This asymmetry between past and future began to concern scientists as a result of the work of two scientific giants of the nineteenth century, James Clerk Maxwell (1831–1879) and Ludwig Boltzmann (1844–1906), who developed reductionistic statistical explanations of gas temperature and pressure. These explanations relied on the presumption that the large-scale regularities, say of heat exchange, were due to each molecule's obedience to Newton's laws of motion, which were explicitly nonstatistical. Hence they hit upon a very accurate and intellectually elegant means of explaining regularities of the whole in terms of the mechanical behavior of the parts.

In a brilliant combination of established principles of statistical reasoning and a still unproven atomism, Maxwell, Boltzmann, and other statistical physicists suggested that thermal energy (heat) in a gas was the straightforward effect of, or in fact identical to, kinetic energy (energy of motion). So the macroscopic properties of heat and pressure could be explained by mechanical laws of motion governing individual particles. The faster the molecules were moving, the greater the heat of the gas, and the greater the pressure (because the molecules were banging more energetically into the sides of the container).

However, since no one could conceivably observe and measure the motions of these smallest particles, their properties must be inferred from observable properties of the collective they comprised. In developing the kinetic theory of gases, Boltzmann and Maxwell postulated that heat was (a function of?) the sum kinetic energy of the randomly moving molecules in the system being measured. Heat transfer from a hotter region to a colder one was a transfer of this kinetic energy.

Using a liquid instead of a gaseous example, the nature of the kinetic theory of heat transfer might be illustrated well. As my cup of tea cools, the higher average kinetic energy of the tea molecules is transferred to the surrounding air, whose molecules are not moving as quickly. These air molecules, whose random motions' kinetic energy defines room temperature, are sped up in the immediate vicinity of the tea. As the fast-moving tea molecules impact the slower air molecules, the tea molecules lose some of their speed and fall beneath the surface, making way for more energetic tea molecules to rise to the interface with the air and suffer the same sinking fate.

Now we are in a position to describe why predictions offered in these sciences are fuzzy. Since some energy is lost to the environment in each collision, the cup of tea will eventually reach room temperature, as the tea molecules and room air molecules reach thermodynamic equilibrium. The tea will no longer be hot tea. Or will it? Confining our considerations to the simple "tea room air" system, the second law of thermodynamics requires that the tea will lose heat to the room, until the average kinetic energy of particles in all regions in the room is the same. But what sort of "law" is this? Is it a law in the sense supposed by the Newtonians, where expected behaviors are required? Does this law say that it is impossible, for instance, that rather than the tea cooling to room temperature, the tea will not spontaneously get hotter? Because the laws of thermodynamics, interpreted via the kinetic theory, are statistical—that is, based on the presumption of randomly moving particles—it cannot be strictly necessary that the system evolve as expected. There is no law, then, that requires any speedy molecule to collide with a more lethargic one and thus sacrifice some of its energy. So is there a lawfulness that governs the collective, but not the component parts? It would seem so, but only if our definition of "law" undergoes serious adjustment. This becomes a problem for reductionistic explanations in general, since the collective behavior can never be exhaustively explained in terms of the component parts, if those parts behave in inexplicable ways.

It is a truism to say that it is highly probable that the most probable distribution of kinetic energies of the molecules will be reached. But we cannot say that the most probable state *must* be reached. There is a non-zero probability that my tea will not cool down. Analogously, there is a non-zero probability that no Frenchmen will commit suicide next year. Since every Frenchman is presumably free to choose life, it is possible that every one will do so. Yet the statistical stability of suicide rates convinces us to near certainty that some will choose the deadly alternative. But no rational person would presume to analyze any individual Frenchman and predict with confidence his self-destruction within a year. But if the statistical regularities exist solely because of mechanical necessity of component parts, then our inability to predict individual fates is only due to our ignorance of relevant causal factors, and such predictions are theoretically possible. So some unfortunate persons, on this reading, are in fact destined for suicide, even though we do not know it. So statistical predictions, such as one claiming that a certain number of bank robberies will happen next year, one that does not specify which robbers or which banks, is a fuzzy prediction. There seems to be no accessible mechanical reason why the prediction might not be drastically wrong. Maybe next year no one will rob banks. The major question whether these mechanical explanations are merely inaccessible, or absent altogether, is tied directly to questions about the value and scope of reductionistic thinking.

Criticizing statistical predictions because they are not quite certain is often called "nit-picking" or "quibbling." Someone might say, "Sure, there is a slight chance that no one will rob a bank next year, but that probability is so low that it is not worth serious consideration. Maybe we can't be sure, but I'll put my money on the statistical prediction." This response is quintessentially Peircean. What matters is a future practical situation. My belief is precisely my intention to act in a certain way. This is not the same as mathematical certainty, even though our confidence is high that someone, somewhere will rob a bank. This kind of confidence short of certainty is reflected in the life and philosophy of David Hume, who maintained that all of our beliefs are commitments to something like statistical generalizations. He doubted that causal connections in nature could ever be shown, but he played billiards and did not repeatedly burn his hands in fires to test his skepticism. Maybe he couldn't be sure that the fire would burn him next time, but he would bet on it. For Peirce and many of his followers, this "bet" illustrates the essential nature of human believing, which is inescapably directed toward an uncertain, changeable, undetermined, and fuzzy future.

Notes

[1] As reported by Diogenes Laertius, recorded in Forrest Baird and Walter Kaufmann, eds., *Ancient Philosophy*, 2d ed. (Upper Saddle River NJ: Prentice-Hall, 1997) 40.

[2] Joseph Brent, *Charles Sanders Peirce: A Life* (Bloomington IN: Indiana University Press, 1993) 3.

[3] CP 6:39.

[4] CP 6.11.

[5] CP 6.201.

[6] CP 6.36.

[7] CP 1.323.

[8] CP 6.61.

[9] CP 1.174.

For Further Reading

Brent, Joseph. *Charles Sanders Peirce: A Life*. Bloomington IN: Indiana University Press, 1993.

Hacking, Ian. *The Taming of Chance*. Cambridge: Cambridge University Press, 1990.

Lucas, J. R. *The Concept of Probability*. Oxford: Clarendon Press, 1970.

Peterson, Ivars. *The Jungles of Randomness: A Mathematical Safari*. New York: John Wiley & Sons, Inc., 1998.

Faith and the Fuzzy Future

Chapter 4

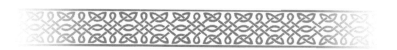

The young man stood trembling in his stricken stillness, frozen in space and time in front of the packed church sanctuary. In the matter of only a few seconds, several months replayed themselves in his mind, in seemingly exhaustive detail. These were the few seconds before he would see his bride-to-be appear at the far end of the center aisle. These were the few seconds before he would pledge his life, in front of the crowd, God, and his mother-in-law, to faithful partnership with a young woman he had known for only a small percentage of his young life.

He flashed back to the day he decided to offer an engagement ring, the same day he informed his best friend of the plan, and the same day the best friend urgently implored him not to do it. That advice had stung, but that friend now stood near, the ceremonial best man. The groom flashed back to the dozens of others, who also without the benefit of knowing the bride, had offered the same counsel. So many of those had related how happy they had been before marriage, but how marriage had suffocated that happiness and extinguished the dreams of their youth.

The interrogative refrain posed by countless questioners during those months echoed in an endless mental feedback loop: "Are you sure? Are you really sure you're ready?" His consistent answer to that query entered the loop: "No, I'm not sure. How could anyone expect to be sure?" That answer sounded good in the prenuptial weeks and months, but now it took on a new, unanticipated gravity. He wasn't really sure. So why was he standing here amid flowers and the organ prelude feigning confidence? Such was the tumult in his soul that he was unaware of the flowers, the music, the wedding party, and even the assembled guests.

But just as the crescendo of anxiety was about to overwhelm him, the crescendo of the magnificent Mendelssohn wedding march broke through to seize his attention. Simultaneously a beatific vision appeared in the foyer at the end of the aisle. Like a glorious sunrise dispersing the clouds at dawn, his beloved began her deliberate journey toward the altar. He knew that he was doing the right thing, that this place, right now, was the only place in the world for him. The flashback gave way to a glorious immersion in the present moment, filled to abundance with expectation of a magical future. He almost felt as if he could predict that future, and he knew that he could commit himself to it.

As human beings, the future is enormously important to us, even formative of what we are. Yet we cannot get a grip on it. We can't predict it or even think about it clearly. Yet we define ourselves as we direct our deepest convictions toward it. This profound lack of understanding about the future is a fundamental contributor to the end of certainty, and the resulting uncertainty can be the beginning of faith if we will but trust. The young man did not know what the future of his marriage would bring, yet he was willing to commit himself to act in a particular manner anyway. Such is the nature of covenant.

This chapter will follow what might appear to be a circuitous route, from natural science to Peirce's theory of meaning, to existentialism, and back to natural science again. At the end two things should be abundantly clear: that the future is an indispensable part of all of our thinking, scientific or otherwise, and that this future is irreducibly fuzzy (at least to human reason). Thus, if we are persons with any kind of faith commitment to this fuzzy future, we must keep on working out our salvation with fear and trembling. Whether we be philosophers, scientists, saints, sinners, or the humblest believers in anything at all, we stand at the precipice, transfixed yet inspired at the risky projects that will define the only self we have. We may, like Pierre Simon de Laplace, find comfort in the belief that a clockwork underlies it all, that everything must happen just the way it does. But beware comfortable beliefs, for they often become the most perilous of all.

Reason, Science, and Prediction

Rational thought has a long history of seeking to make predictions. In an episode lauded as an early triumph of reason over superstition, the ancient Greek thinker Thales predicted an eclipse. He recognized regular patterns in nature that others failed to see and provided an explanation of eclipses in general that did not rely on the capricious mood swings of the Hellenic pantheon. Apparently by careful observation of the changing positions of the sun and moon, Thales could tell, some time before the event, that the moon would obscure the midday sun one day in May of 585 BCE. Legend has it that people were amazed at his clairvoyance and thought him some kind of seer or wizard with occult powers. This assessment by the masses was not entirely off the mark, as "clairvoyance" means, etymologically, "the ability to see clearly." "Seer" denotes one who can peer accurately into the future. Thales could see more clearly into the future than most of his contemporaries and won for himself a place on the list of ancient sages.

This recognition of pattern in what was thought to be a rather chaotic spirit-infested universe was the beginning of Western philosophy. It began a movement of pattern-finding that continues into the modern world. Modern science, in particular, has been a highly successful chapter in this saga in the West. When Galileo, Descartes, Leibniz, Newton, and other early modern thinkers began to quantify the patterns, naming them with the precise language of mathematics, many thought that this pattern-discovery quest had reached its pinnacle. Since knowing the patterns allowed both prediction and explanation, the universe seemed susceptible to a mathematical accounting. Pierre Simon de Laplace was among the most impressed with the potential of this new science to predict with ever-increasing precision.

He envisioned a hypothetical intelligence, later dubbed "Laplace's demon," who, armed with knowledge of Newton's laws of motion and the current positions and motions of all particles in the universe, could predict all future states of affairs. In his own words (translated from the French),

Given for one instant an intelligence which could comprehend all the forces by which nature is animated and the respective situation of the beings who compose it—an intelligence sufficiently vast to submit these data to analysis—it would embrace in the same formula the movements of the greatest bodies of the universe and those of the lightest atom; for it, nothing would be uncertain and the future, as the past, would be present to its eyes.[1]

Clearly, Laplace is "exhibit A" in Peirce's category of necessitarians. These remarks of Laplace, ironically, come at the beginning of his landmark book *A Philosophical Essay on Probabilities*. This is ironic because the success and growth of theories of probability is largely responsible for the movement away from the very necessitarianism championed by Laplace and thousands of others. Though he was a leading figure in the development of probability theory, he always saw the use of probability as a concession to human ignorance of precise detail in a system. These details he presumed to be entirely deterministic, proceeding according to Newton's inexorable laws of motion. Since humans cannot gather and process sufficient data to create precise and certain predictions, we must settle for probabilistic predictions, which become all but certain when involving large numbers. This view, which denied any inherently random events, was the majority position so vigorously rebuked by Peirce. Later we will address probability theory and the nature and extent of its predictive powers. For now, remember that for many scientific reductionists, like Laplace, the magic of natural science was the way in which the future is encoded in the equations of today.

The Meaning in the Future

Clearly from the earliest emergence of thinking that might be classed "scientific," such thinking has had an obvious future orientation. Even those who gave birth to the sciences of chance established their scientific status by championing the predictive ability of the new methods. Charles Peirce would radically expand this notion of future-dependence by arguing powerfully that scientific and factual utterances were fundamentally constituted by reference to the future. Any claim I make that purports to describe a world will contain ideas that cannot be understood apart from their reference to a potential future practical situation. This notion of Peirce's, which came to be the fountainhead of American pragmatism, is most succinctly (if not most clearly) stated thus: "Consider what effects, that might conceivably have practical bearings, we conceive the object of our conception to have. Then, our conception of these effects is the whole of our conception of the object."[2] This unfortunately obtuse locution might be better stated: "Our conception of any object of thought is exactly our conception of the practical effects that this object might conceivably have." In other words, the entire content of any conception I entertain is my conception of its practical consequences (hence "pragmatism").[3] Therefore, this is a theory about meaning, one that was influenced by Peirce's close acquaintance with the sciences, but that he saw as fundamental to all speech and cognition, not just the branch usually called "science."

He uses the example of a diamond's hardness to illustrate his point. To claim that a diamond is hard is to claim that when one experiences it in contact with other substances, they, and not it, will be scratched. So our idea of its hardness is precisely our expectation that it will scratch and not be scratched. This does not mean that we must actually attempt to scratch diamonds in order for our concept of their hardness to be meaningful. His maxim simply describes the content of the conception as expectations of a potential practical future. "Practical" effects, for Peirce and other pragmatists, must be potentially detectable by the senses, and thus at least potentially accessible to other persons with similar sense organs. So claims that have no possible future practical effects are then devoid of meaning for Peirce. He uses the Catholic doctrine of transubstantiation as an example of such a claim, the belief that the wine and bread blessed for Holy Communion actually become the blood and body of Christ. Used strictly as a logical example, Peirce notes,

> We can consequently mean nothing by wine but what has certain effects, direct or indirect, upon our senses; and to talk of something as having all the sensible characters of wine, yet being in reality blood, is senseless jargon.[4]

Every difference must make a difference. So a disagreement whose final resolution makes no conceivable difference is empty. Protestants and Catholics alike agree, according to Peirce, on the sensible effects of the experience of wine and bread, hence there can be no actual disagreement.

It is foolish for Catholics and Protestants to fancy themselves in disagreement about the elements of the sacrament, if they agree in regard
to all their sensible effects, here and hereafter.[5]

Presumably, however, if they did disagree about the possible sensible
effects of, say, drinking wine that was blessed for communion and drinking wine that was not, then there could be a real issue between them.
Peirce challenges his readers to try to imagine what the contents of
their conceptions might be, if his view is incorrect. All of our beliefs are
but habits of mind, preparing us for a potential future practical encounter
of one kind or another. Any other alleged content seems unable to gain
intellectual traction. For instance, traditional correspondence theories of
truth usually presumed that human minds possessed propositions like an
encyclopedia possessed facts, a fixed and changeless catalog of factual
claims. Some of these were true, if they corresponded to the "way things
really are." Others failed to correspond, and hence were false. Peirce was
impressed at the practical emptiness of these conceptions of meaning and
truth. Given the kind of thinking we actually do, our beliefs are never fixed
and changeless in some abstract mathematical space (recall how thinking
happens with signs, discussed in chapter 2). In addition, we can never
hope to "match up" our ideas with some kind of "God's-eye-view" of the
universe as it is. We will always do our thinking at a distance from whatever "truly is the case," and wonder if our catalog of propositions matches
God's, on this traditional account of meaning. Even if God tells us which
propositions correspond to reality and which do not, we must still adjust
our beliefs according to whether or not we think we are perceiving this
instruction aright. As long as our thinking operates in the way that it does,
here or hereafter, we must always admit the possibility that we might be
shown to be mistaken, in the future. As long as our thinking works the
way that it does now, each must decide if the claims that the God's-eye-
view has been given to us are trustworthy, and even then we might be
wrong (by perhaps believing a claim of divine authority to be authentic
when we are in fact being deceived by some sinister force). Even in these
speculative cases it is hard to get away from the fact that our beliefs are
directed even *now* toward a *then* that will serve to confirm or disconfirm
the belief.

In the West we interpret confirmations of our beliefs as evidence of their timeless truth. When beliefs are disconfirmed, we call them false. But a belief accepted at any time might later come to be rejected, and access to a timeless truth is not in the province of human conviction or logic. We may claim that some propositions are true for all time, but claiming such does not make it so. All of our beliefs take the form of signs, usually in the form of linguistic expressions, and these can never decisively be shown to correspond to any fixed thing-in-itself. The signs themselves are evolving, being adjusted and replaced by similar signs in a perpetual process. The most we can say is that a belief that comes to be borne out by practical experience is one that will be retained until such a time as it is no longer borne out. All the time the content of the belief is exactly the expectation of that future time when the belief will either be borne out or not.

Peirce's view of the radical future-orientedness of all concepts is controversial, and here is not the place to present a full-blown defense of his sign-based reading of the universe. But his ideas have been enormously fruitful and accepted by great numbers of thinkers, especially in the United States. Even if his contention that the whole of the meaning of any conception lies in practical future effects is ultimately overstated, he at least has a point in suggesting that our everyday knowledge claims are heavily invested in future expectations. Thus all of our knowing has much in common with the scientific modes that emphasize predictions and tests. Whether I say "Pluto will be in position X on January 1," or "Joe is lazy," I am expressing a meaning that presumes a potential future practical effect. I am saying that if I look through a telescope aimed at position X on January 1, I will see Pluto, and that if I expect Joe to show strong initiative in the case I assign him a task, then I will be disappointed. This is the root meaning of each of these claims, and each retains its meaning even if I never again peer through a telescope or never again encounter Joe. "Modern science" is not unique in imbuing its knowledge claims with a heavy dose of the future. Peirce sees all claims as future-referenced, and in this logic-inspired conclusion he would find a very unlikely set of allies in the existentialists, who also make the future a central element of human knowing and being.

The Human Project

From very different personal and philosophical starting points, Peirce and the existentialists came to remarkably similar conclusions about human nature and human meaning. Peirce, Martin Heidegger (1889–1976), and Jean-Paul Sartre (1905–1980) all saw the unsteadiness and wonder of the human self as rooted in its unavoidable investment in the future. Of course they were concerned with different angles of the problems of human meaning, but the fact that they came to very comparable conclusions from largely antagonistic starting points can tell us much about the nature of the end of certainty and give us clues as to where to go from here. Much of the shared outcome of these two very different camps was anticipated early in the nineteenth century by Søren Kierkegaard, whose relevance to issues of certainty and faith will be addressed near the end of our study.

For the existentialists, the particular kind of existence experienced by humans is irrevocably characterized by care. It is of the essence of human existence to care, according to Heidegger, about how things turn out. Heidegger expresses it this way:

> Because it is primordially constituted by care, any *Dasein* [the human kind of existence] is already ahead of itself. As being, it has in every case already projected itself upon definite possibilities of its existence . . .[6]

Stated less Heidegger-like, this means that since humans are essentially beings who care about something, they are always focusing themselves toward future possibilities. One implication of this feature of human existence is that it leaves us (at least partly) undefined at the present moment. If our selves are (at least partly) constituted by a projection into the "not yet," then this leaves a kind of empty space in our "now selves." A similar idea is advocated by a successor and follower of Heidegger, the famous existentialist Jean-Paul Sartre. Sartre believes that our orientation toward the future creates a profound emptiness at the heart of the human person. This situation, for a number of reasons, creates anxiety in free creatures. This anxiety is partly created from the fact that, being free, our future is not yet fixed.

A couple of terms from the Heidegger passage invite further investigation. He says that *Dasein* is "already ahead of itself." At any given time a human, because he or she is constituted essentially by care, is ahead of itself. What a person is *now* is shot through with what the person would be tomorrow, and forever. Because we are free and because we care, we live in the future. But also because we are free, that future is not fixed. It has no definite shape or obvious existence. But because we care, we "project" ourselves into that realm of the not-yet. So we are ahead of ourselves because we are, primordially, our projects. The double-meaning of this word, "project," in English is fortunate, because each meaning reveals a key element in the existential structure of a person. "Project," the verb, means "to thrust outward or forward." As a noun, the most common meaning is "an endeavor requiring a concerted effort." In both senses we humans *are* our projects. As we build toward our endeavors small and large, applying concerted efforts to reach our goals, we are defining ourselves by thrusting ourselves forward into a future that we will help make. We are now what we are creating ourselves to be, which is not yet. This situation is highly paradoxical and more than a little bit troubling. But without our projects, we would have nothing to care about, hence we would not be *Dasein*, we would not be human.

This understanding of the future as a component part of the now for *Dasein* leads to a conception of time that is quite different from that usually employed in physical sciences. Time does not flow in a homogeneous fashion for human beings. Evenly ticking clock time in which each second counts exactly one second is not the time used to note succession in a being who cares. For Heidegger, past, present, and future are richly entangled elements of any "now" for *Dasein*. For beings like ourselves, neither the future nor the past can be excised from the present moment. They are different ways of looking at who we are. One future event that is part of who we are now is our death. We are beings-toward-death, and this creates a situation unique to *Dasein*. The future is uncertain, except for death. Hence our projects, which define our very being, will apparently come to an end. Humans are unique on the planet in their awareness of their own demise. We are aware of no other creature that knows it is going to die. This mindfulness of the end, always at least in the background of our thoughts, colors our conception of time. The future is not like the past.

French existentialist Jean-Paul Sartre shares much of Heidegger's perspective. For Sartre, human beings are fundamentally free, which means that they continually make themselves. This, too, requires a future-orientation. Each decision that a free being makes is a step into an unknown and open future, and these steps make each human being who he or she is. The paradoxes of this way of speaking must not be lost on us. If each of us is a self that chooses itself, we are never quite a self. Since there is always already the next choice to be made, the self is yet to be formed. This is every bit as impossible as lifting yourself up by your own bootstraps. Hence there is an unavoidable nothingness, a lack, at the center of the human person. This complete freedom, for Sartre, creates a kind of dizziness, inducing nausea. We always find ourselves in some concrete situation that is no longer amenable to our choosing, facing a future that we will make. Sartre characterizes this aspect of human existence in a picturesque fashion:

> Man first of all is the being who hurls himself toward a future and who is conscious of imagining himself as being in the future. Man is at the start a plan which is aware of itself, rather than a patch of moss, a piece of garbage, or a cauliflower . . .[7]

If you are a plan that is aware of itself, then you are always already bringing the future into the present, since those projects toward which you commit yourself are the essence of what you are. But since you are always making yourself, your commitments and projects are subject to change.

A couple of simple illustrations will help to illuminate Sartre's (and Heidegger's) point. We are accustomed to hearing of the ethical importance of keeping one's word. The habit of keeping one's word is a necessary condition of integrity. The cultivation of this habit is fundamentally an intention to carry forth a particular kind of project in a potential future experience. If I tell you that I will rise to the nation's defense in time of war or if I promise to pick up a loaf of bread on the way home from work, then, being a man of my word means that I have a plan (or "am" a plan, if my word defines me) of action for the future. Our conception of a person's "character" is empty if not constituted largely by that person's future plans and projects. A person of integrity can be counted on to act responsibly in the future; the person without integrity cannot.

When I fail to live up to my word, I feel a deep sense of loss. More troubling still is the sense of not having a project at all. Most people can identify with the letdown that follows the accomplishment of a major life goal. If you devote the majority of your energies toward a major achievement and then accomplish it, there is also a sense of loss (along with whatever sense of accomplishment that might be present). This experience bears a formal resemblance to postpartum depression, when the anticipation of the arrival of a child, a future-orientation that shapes life itself for months, gives way to the reality of the child. The all-absorbing obsession with a specific future event is now gone. Similar experiences are reported in the landing of a big account, graduating from college or graduate school, and completing a dissertation. All of these examples are testimony to how much our projections into the future mean to us. The King James translation of Proverbs 29:18 expresses this idea tersely and memorably: "Where there is no vision, the people perish."

This vision of the future, our "prophetic" bearing, the "not-yet" of personhood is its crowning glory and its insidious curse. It is at the same time the precondition of sin and the staging ground for faith. It is at the heart of existing as persons, and the sin-revealed awareness of our nakedness before God. God and the serpent each supplied a vision of the future for Adam and Eve. They chose knowledge, not believing that it would bring death, a death promised by God. We, too, choose knowledge of good and evil and try to fix our tack into the future from this inevitable, yet fallen perspective. Faith will be impossible for us until we use those new eyes, opened by the forbidden fruit mysteriously created for us by God to see that we are naked. The modern world, like all other eras, is replete with maneuvers designed to disguise this nakedness from our own eyes. Our powerful aversion to exposure and vulnerability gives rise to dreams of protection and certainty. Our math and logic are illusory fortresses against a God of history if they are ever thought to provide refuge from the contingencies of that history. Dreams of certainty would collapse our future, the arena in which we must forever work out our salvation, into a still and lifeless equation, clean and sterile, leaving no room for the infectious faith of our fathers. But many champions of an air-tight logical account of past and future are now being confronted with a chancy future.

This scientific recognition of a chancy future is no defection, but a growing realization that the work of scientists, logicians, and mathematicians is a human work, undertaken for the same basic reasons and utilizing the same human tools, as everything from parenting to poetry. So let us take a look again at nineteenth-century physical science and Peirce the mathematical logician for corroboration of Sartre's contention that if the future is "recorded in heaven, . . . then it would really no longer be a future."[8] A future recorded in the equations, likewise, would not really be a future.

The Fuzzy Future

We have already seen that Peirce rejected the deterministic philosophy of those who insisted on mechanical necessity in nature. Part of the reason for this rejection was the stubborn fact that experiments refused to match the predictions made by the equations. They were pretty close, sometimes very close, but rarely were they precisely accurate. The attempt to describe actual physical reality with numbers was remarkably helpful, very practical, and even life-saving, but the numbers usually were not precisely descriptive of the systems they sought to depict. The necessitarians presumed this deviation from expectations to be due solely to human limitations in the observation and measurement processes. They thought, with Laplace, that if there were an intelligence capable enough to consider all influences with complete precision, then these deviations would disappear before its analysis. The future would be "recorded" in the equations.

Peirce had a different understanding of the utility of mathematical accounts of natural processes. Staking his claim in a particular school of thought in philosophy of mathematics, Peirce reveals his understanding of numbers: "That part of my solution is that Quantity is merely the mathematician's idealization of meaningless vocables invented for the experimental testing of orders of sequence."[9] He is well aware of how useful numbers are in providing a more accurate account of nature, but he resists the idea that natural entities can be unambiguously quantified. So how good are our numbers? Peirce contends,

> To one who is behind the scenes, and knows that the most refined comparisons of masses, lengths, and angles, far surpassing in precision all other measurements, yet fall behind the accuracy of bank accounts, and that the ordinary determinations of physical constants, such as appear from month to month in the journals, are about on a par with an upholsterer's measurements of carpets and curtains, the idea of mathematical exactitude being demonstrated in the laboratory will appear simply ridiculous.[10]

Peirce, of course, was behind the scenes and worked meticulously to maximize precision in his experiments with gravitational force and other quantities. The kind of exactitude presumed by the necessitarians to prevail in the natural world was not evident to him. Moreover, "any statement to the effect that a certain continuous quantity has a certain exact value, if well founded at all, must be founded on something other than observation."[11] Bank accounts (at least in his day) did not treat continuous variables, but agreed on what the smallest unit must be. Since all agreed that the penny is the basic unit, then the calculations could be exact. In the physical sciences there was no such agreement (and there still is not). Equations "fit" nature well, but not perfectly. The experiments often deviate from expected values. The future continues to harbor surprises.

For Peirce, and for many later thinkers, this lack of fit was no mere phantom of our ignorance of the precise units, but a clue to the absence of such units. For him, it made no sense to speak of a natural "penny" that, once discovered, would confer precision to our predictions. Nature admits continuous variables whose precise and complete identification would require infinite symbolic representation. So for Peirce, the future fails to live up to our expectations because it is intrinsically open. Discrete units will not be found that can describe this continuous world. So the future is fuzzy to any being whose powers of thought are even remotely akin to ours.

Since this world that admits continuous variation is growing and developing and since this makes the future really distinct from the past, maybe the very best snapshot possible of the future is out of focus. On this view of the future, even an ideal time machine/camera that tried to take a picture of the world on a day ten years hence would only produce a very fuzzy image, with only broad shapes and colors visible. The further in the future, the fuzzier the image would be. Only the past has crystallized into actuality; thus we do not become anxious trying to change it. Instead our care is directed toward those indeterminate images whose ultimate contours we can help create, those in the fuzzy future.

Peirce's incorporation of the indeterminate future into the heart of his worldview is very favorable to the existentialist reading of the nature of things, even though it originated from the disciplines of logic, mathematics, and physical science, studies often relegated to irrelevance by the existentialist mindset. Maybe Kierkegaard, the Christian creator of many of the existentialist notions discussed above, was too quick to excoriate math and science; maybe he could have included these practices among authentic human enterprises had he lived long enough to digest the Peircean perspective.

Conclusions

Early modern natural scientists thought that their methods could theoretically lead to certainty. This hope could apparently be justified by the incredible precision of the predictions constructed from mathematical models. The rough edges of the predictions, though, came to be seen by some thinkers as irremediable. These rough edges may in fact be due to the very nature of the future that the sciences would seek to foretell. This future-orientedness, which most agree is central to the sciences, threatens to ruin the dreams of certainty. Moreover, the future is a part of all of our knowledge claims and all of our projects, scientific and otherwise. So if its fuzziness is real and irreducible, then none of our endeavors is free from the uncertainty thus created.

The words of world-renowned American physicist Richard Feynman (1918–1988) summarize well these main points about science's uncertainty and its reliance on prediction. As he said in a 1963 lecture series, scientific conclusions "are guesses as to what is going to happen, and you cannot know what will happen, because you have not made the most complete experiments."[12] And "the laws are guessed; they are extrapolations into the unknown. You do not know what is going to happen, so you take a guess."[13] To guess what will happen is to take a risky look into the future. Feynman believes that "Knowledge is of no real value if all you can tell me is what happened yesterday,"[14] and this is a key reason why "all scientific knowledge is uncertain."[15]

Among the many contributions modern science has made to our way of looking at the universe, central is its reminder of the importance of future expectations in the theories of today. This proleptic invasion of the not-yet into the right-now is corroborated by widely divergent schools and thinkers, specifically the concrete human life of the existentialists and the mathematical logic of Charles Peirce. The future inevitably colors what we know now and who we are now. But the future, for all of the reasons we have discussed above (and others), is very fuzzy to us. This future that comprises so much of our current knowledge necessarily introduces a profound uncertainty into that knowledge. Engaging the fuzzy future with confidence and authenticity, from whatever starting points and for whatever reasons, requires a remarkable investment of faith, the substance of things hoped for.

The leap of faith taken by the bride and the bridegroom was the establishment of a covenant, their trust in each other for the substance of things hoped for. Neither had the luxury of a clear snapshot of life in the future, but if they had, there would have been no need for promise or covenant between them. The marriage bond has provided a powerful metaphor for Christ's relationship to the church since the earliest days of Christianity, and it provides a powerful and related metaphor for human value and knowledge more generally.

Following Peirce, the beliefs that we hold are our action plans for the future. Whether the belief be about the hardness of a diamond or the faithfulness of a spouse, the content of the belief is nothing other than the expectations it engenders with regard to potential future practical situations. I believe that diamonds will scratch other things; I believe that my wife and I will love each other "til death do us part." In neither case does the future invoked by the belief present itself to me with complete clarity, but diamonds are pretty set in their ways, so their futures are more certain. A marriage relationship is much more changeable and flexible, complex and unpredictable than a diamond. So the promises we make to each other are riskier, much more interesting, and infinitely more meaningful than any expectation about the behavior of a rock.

We have staked a lot in our mutual promise to love and cherish without ever seeing the end. It is likewise with our promises to serve God. We think we have it right, but we cannot be sure because we cannot see what we will do in the future. We believe that "God was in Christ, reconciling the world to himself." This means, in part, that we plan to exercise our energies in the ministry of reconciliation in any future practical situation where the opportunity presents itself. Without this practical commitment, this confession of faith would be nothing but empty words; it would not be belief. But those future situations are profoundly unknown to us now. So we work out our salvation in fear and trembling, journeying in the faith that nothing can separate us from the love of Christ. If we had a clear snapshot of the future, there would be no need for covenant. This is why the end of certainty is the beginning of faith. As modernity's dreams of certainty dissolve all around us, in logic and mathematics, in science and philosophy, we are entering an era ripe for an explosion of authentic faith, but we must not forget that all times of great opportunity are times of great risk.

Peirce's understanding of language, belief, chance, and the future can help faith find a foothold as science continues to teach us more about the world and at the same time uncovers greater regions of uncertainty. Peirce can help us see that in our lives as scientists and as believers we often do the same things. Whether in the church, the lab, or the study, we hold beliefs that are given content by a future that is not well known to us, and we plan our encounters, both big and small, according to those beliefs, those habits of mind. Insofar as the beliefs are borne out by our individual and collective experience, they will be retained and strengthened. But if future testing shows a belief to be found wanting, if it fails us in navigating our individual and collective futures, then the belief or mental habit must change. This understanding of the nature of belief works very well in a world where science continues to reveal microscopic indeterminacy, spontaneous habit-taking in physics and chemistry, the developmental nature of life forms, and the inescapable "embodiedness" of human experience. We now turn to those scientific studies that provide us with new and challenging beliefs and underline the end of certainty. With Peirce's help, we can see how these developments are indeed friendly to a courageous and fulfilling faith.

Notes

[1]Pierre Simon de Laplace, *A Philosophical Essay on Probabilities*, trans. Frederick Lincoln Emory and Frederick William Truscott (New York: Dover Publications, Inc., 1951) 4.

[2]CP 5.402.

[3]The term apparently was coined by William James, who credited the basic idea to Peirce. Peirce felt that the notion of pragmatism had begun to take on popular meanings he had not intended, so he renamed his own ideas about the meanings of concepts "pragmaticism."

[4]CP 5.401.

[5]Ibid.

[6]*Being and Time,* trans. John MacQuarrie and Edward Robinson (New York: Harper and Row, 1962) 363.
[7]*Existentialism and Human Emotions* (New York: Philosophical Library, 1957) 16.
[8]Ibid., 23-24.
[9]CP 4.154.
[10]CP 6.44.
[11]Ibid.
[12]Richard P. Feynman, *The Meaning of It All: Thoughts of a Citizen-Scientist* (Reading MA: Addison-Wesley, 1998) 26.
[13]Ibid., 24.
[14]Ibid., 25.
[15]Ibid., 26.

For Further Reading

Feynman, Richard. *The Meaning of It All: The Thoughts of a Citizen-Scientist.* Reading MA: Addison-Wesley, 1998.

Kosko, Bart. *Fuzzy Thinking: The New Science of Fuzzy Logic.* New York: Hyperion, 1993.

MacQuarrie, John. *Existentialism.* New York: Penguin Books, 1972.

Oaklander, L. Nathan. *Existentialist Philosophy: An Introduction.* Englewood Cliffs NJ: Prentice-Hall, Inc., 1992.

Sartre, Jean Paul. *Existentialism and Human Emotions.* New York: Philosophical Library, 1957.

Chapter 5

Quantum
Leaps and Limits

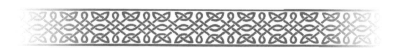

Your perfectly struck 6-iron shot sailed up the hill toward the green whose surface you could not see due to its elevation. It seemed to be drawn right toward the top of the flagstick, which you could see. After you ascend the hill to discover a putting surface barren of golf balls, two visions compete for your imagination. The ball might be nestled in the hole for a rare eagle two, or it might have ended up in the sand trap beyond the green. You don't yet know in which place it lies, but you know that it is one place or the other, since you can see the rest of the terrain and nothing can be in two places at once. You know that nothing you do now, such as looking in the hole, will have any effect on where the ball actually is. You know this because you have some awareness of the laws of nature that dictate the motion of the ball once it has left the clubface and that once it starts on its way, its path is determined by physics.

If you were playing a super-microscopic round of golf, using, say, an electron instead of a golf ball, you would know none of these things. Your electron-ball might be in an intermediate state of hole/trap at the same time, residing simultaneously in both places and neither, until you check. Your act of looking for it may cause it to drop either in the trap or in the hole, though you can't predict which. You also have no idea what trajectory it followed to arrive where it is. It had an equal chance of following any one of the possible paths open to it and maybe followed more than one. You don't know because the electron-ball is not compelled to follow Newton's laws of motion. You know the probability of its having followed any available path and the probability that it will be found either in the trap or in the hole, but that is all.

Readers familiar with physics or the philosophy of physics should be quite irritated by that last paragraph because it is loaded with errors and may appear to be headed down that road to Never-Never Land traveled by scores of "interpreters" of quantum mechanics. Let me assure those and other readers that the errors are there for a purpose that will become clear by the end of this chapter. Quantum theory doesn't tell us anything we can apply directly to the philosophy of golf, religious experience, God, mysticism, or Eastern religions. But it does show us that the assumptions at the root of the conceptual confusions of the last paragraph are deeply mistaken. Anything like that quantum-golf experience could happen only if electrons bore any relevant resemblance to golf balls. Classical physics, that dominant worldview of the West, champion of mathematical certainty, fostered by the likes of Descartes, Galileo, and Newton, took for granted that there would be relevant similarities between golf balls and the invisibly tiny particles that compose them. The extraordinarily successful mechanical philosophy of Newton rested upon the universality of certain kinds of properties and laws. Essential to his way of thinking, and that of his intellectual heirs, was the assumption that the properties of middle-sized, stable, (apparently) simple objects (MSSOs), and the rules governing their behavior, applied to things other than MSSOs, all the way down to the smallest components of matter. Quantum mechanics vigorously uproots that assumption and thus destabilizes an entire way of looking at the world.

The Birth of the Quantum

On October 14, 1900, an academician presented a paper at a conference. He offered his thoughts on how to solve a perplexing problem in his field. The same thing probably happened somewhere on October 15, and yesterday and today. A vanishingly small percentage of these papers end up ever being noticed again. Many of these papers are nothing more than educated guesses (and some are not even very educated!); but when quandaries persist year after year, even a stab in the dark is welcomed by the academic community. Max Planck's October paper was something like an educated stab in the dark. Planck suggested that the essence of the paper was really nothing more than a handy mathematical trick that could be used to account for the way radiation behaves in a heated enclosure. With no physical reason for doing so, he proposed that the energy in the box be considered as if it consisted of tiny packets of a specific size, rather than as a continuous quantity available in any size.[1] Thus was the idea of the "quantum" introduced into physics. With this modest attempt to alleviate calculation problems related to "cavity" radiation, the most controversial and revolutionary movement in modern physics was born. The scientific and philosophical firestorm caused by the quantum has not abated even by the end of the century whose beginning saw its announcement. The scientific explorations begun by Planck in that year have forever changed the landscape not only of physics, but also of human knowing.

Planck's paper did not give the initial appearance of revolution. Planck, the conservative academician, simply thought he was applying the enormously successful computational techniques of statistical mechanics to a different kind of problem, and this as a stop-gap measure. He was convinced (and remained convinced the rest of his life) that his technique was nothing more than a temporary concession to our ignorance about the precise behavior of electromagnetic energy at microscopic scales. In this view he shared the perspective of most practitioners of statistical mechanics, who thought that probabilistic reasoning as it applied to large collections of "atoms" was needed only because we did not know each atom's individual trajectory. Planck saw in statistical explanations a way to predict macroscopic properties of systems even if we did not know much about the microscopic states. Thus by treating (the effects of) electromagnetic energy in the same way that Boltzmann treated particles, predictions about large quantities of these elementary units could be made, and made quite accurately. There was, of course, no reason to think that energy actually existed in these tiny little packets. If it did, then the classical understanding of physics was in deep trouble, and Planck knew it. The last thing he wanted was to be the instigator of the downfall of the Newtonian view of the world.

Within a few years, however, there were compelling physical reasons to believe that the solutions suggested by Planck were much more than a convenient mathematical shortcut. Thanks to the work of Albert Einstein and many others, physicists came to believe that energy did in fact exist only in discrete units and that these units were defined according to Planck's initial calculations.[2] Nature's basic building blocks were not continuous, nor was the energy of their interaction with one another. The classical view of physics, associated with the mechanical philosophy of Isaac Newton, which depicted a natural world describable by continuous mathematical functions, a nature whose basic structure did not require recourse to probabilistic generalization about large numbers of constituent units, was fatally wounded. Planck's guess had exposed something fundamental about the structure of the micro-world, at least insofar as this structure would ever submit to human depictions of it.

Why Is This Such a Weird Idea?

To begin to see why quantization is such an odd notion and why it has led to such philosophical puzzles, a little background is in order. Richard Feynman has said that all of the perplexities of quantum physics can be illustrated by the famous two-slit experiment.[3] Scores of variations of this experiment have been performed as part of the twentieth century's quest to uncover something of the structure of matter and energy. The basic features of the physical behaviors described below have been confirmed over and over again in many different laboratories around the world, though the setup that will be described is a simplified idealization, presented in the interest of clarity. The actual physical experiments that have been performed have yielded tremendous agreement about what will happen when the next such experiment comes along, yet they have generated tremendous controversy about what is "really" going on in the smallest regions of matter. But there is some measure of consensus that we must begin to take seriously three quantum-induced notions that comprise the most powerful threat yet to dreams of scientific certainty: chance, nonlocality, and subjectivity. Furthermore, we will see that, even if these controversial notions turn out not to be fundamental to matter and our knowledge of it, quantum mechanics at least serves as a powerful and apparently incontrovertible reminder of the conclusions of chapter 2—that our descriptions of the world are never precise enough to claim certain and complete knowledge.

The earliest version of the two-slit experiment had nothing to do with quantum theory and was performed almost one hundred years before Planck's paper was presented. It was devised and carried out by English scientist Thomas Young as part of his attempt to demonstrate that light was propagated in waves rather than particles. His conclusions seemed obvious and unarguable and accomplished the near banishment of Isaac Newton's notion that light consisted of particles. Young demonstrated the wave nature of light by aiming a light source at an opaque barrier into which two parallel vertical slits had been cut. These slits allowed light to pass through them and then strike another opaque surface, which we will call a screen (like a movie screen). The image on the screen, formed by the light passing through the two slits, is not what you might expect. You do not see just two bright lines, one corresponding to each slit, but alternating vertical stripes of light and dark. This is called an "interference pattern." It seems that the only way to explain this pattern is to see the light as a wave phenomenon.

The interference pattern occurs because of the influence of the two wave sets, one from each slit, on each other. After passing through the slits (and because the waves originated from the same source and are thus "in phase"), the two sets of waves interfere with one another. Where the wave peaks and troughs coincide with each other, the waves "double up" and create a bright area. Where the peaks and troughs are in opposite orientations (peak to trough and vice versa), the waves "cancel out" and produce a dark area. If light were particles rather than waves, then these particles would rather haphazardly bounce off of each other and two fuzzy images on the screen, with a bright area aligned with each slit, growing consistently dimmer in each direction away from the slit region. Only if light travels in waves can the interference pattern happen. Hence Young, and practically everyone else, became convinced of the wave nature of light.

Later in the nineteenth century, light and many other forms of energy were determined to be wavelike oscillations in the electromagnetic field. Today we understand that light, as well as the waves that heat food in the microwave oven, x-rays, radio waves, and more all are variations in the same field, oscillations varying in wavelength, frequency, and intensity. Thus our eyes are analogous to a radio receiver. Each particular kind of radio receiver is built to receive only certain kinds of signals that are carried in the electromagnetic field. The FM radio cannot pick up AM signals. We cannot see X-rays because their wavelength is too short to be detected by our particular kind of receiver, but we can see light waves, whose wavelengths fall within the range to which our eyes are "tuned." This understanding of the nature of light and other radiation has been remarkably successful, yielding all of the technological wonders that characterize the modern age. Challenges to this view should not be taken lightly. But these waves are usually conceived as continuous, without breaks or interruptions in them. The mathematics that describes them utilizes this presumed continuity. There is nothing about waves themselves that suggests that energy carried in them can only exist in certain quantities. Certainly nature would not be arbitrary enough to prohibit the existence of certain frequencies or their corresponding energy levels. If radiation is not continuous, then there must be something wrong with the wave picture of electromagnetic energy. Planck seemed to believe that the enormous success of this picture would ensure its survival for the ages. But Planck, the classical physicist, had led the way to the dissolution of the classical picture and a revisitation of the classical two-slit experiment would confirm the depth of the disturbance he had caused.

The two-slit experiment seemed to prove that light was a wave. Planck's work led to the suggestion that energy came in discrete packets, quanta, that could only be described statistically. A quantum of light came to be known as a photon and exhibited features we normally associate with a particle rather than a wave. Einstein's discoveries related to the photoelectric effect (in which electrons are scattered from metal foils due to the impact of photons) suggested unambiguously that light existed as particles of a finite size. Light and other forms of energy can only exist as whole number multiples of Planck's constant. This constant is so small that most of our world seems to exhibit continuity, but just as close inspection of even a high-quality newspaper photograph reveals individual dots, so a close look at the microscopic world yields a fundamentally grainy image. But, if this is what nature is like, then there should be no interference effect in the two-slit experiment.

Think of it this way. If we are using a very low intensity laser, it is conceivable that it might emit only one photon at a time in the direction of our two slits, delivering the next one only after the previous one has made its impression on the screen. If this screen is replaced with photographic film, then the (approximate) location of the impact of each photon can be recorded. What happens when we do the experiment in this way? Eventually, after sufficient photons, traveling one at a time, strike the film, we will see the interference pattern. The film will look just like the back screen in Young's 1801 experiment. But how can this happen? There must be interference, one wave combining with another, to produce the light and dark stripes. If photons go through one slit or the other independently, then from where does the interference pattern come? It is not possible for half of a photon to go through each slit, since photons (as with all quanta) cannot be divided. It is not possible that a photon can "know" which part of the screen it is supposed to hit or which slit it is supposed to go through in order to produce the pattern. But the pattern persists. Even more strangely, the pattern persists only as long there are two slits available for the photon to traverse. But how can the presence of a second slit, at the moment the photon passes through the other one, make any difference? If it goes through slit A, then how can it matter whether slit B even exists or not? Once it has entered A, doesn't B become irrelevant? Not exactly.

If we run the same experiment but close one of the slits, the interference pattern disappears. Independent photons do seem to "know" whether there are one or two slits available. Obviously this is absurd since a photon, traveling at the speed of light, cannot be influenced by a slit a few millimeters away that it doesn't even pass through, can it? Moreover, if we try to detect which of the two slits the photon traverses, the interference pattern disappears again. There seems to be some sense in which the presence of the interference pattern depends on our not knowing which slit was "chosen" by the photon. Just by trying to catch a peek at the photon passing, we remove the interference pattern. With both slits open, we presume that any photon making it to the screen had a fifty-fifty chance of going through either slit A or slit B. When this role of chance is removed by our placing some sort of detector next to one of the slits, the interference pattern goes away. We can either know where the photon is (understood as particle) or how a large number interact collectively (understood as wave), but not both.

The inability to know simultaneously these two facts about a photon is one example of the famous quantum mechanical "indeterminacy." The most widely known formulation of indeterminacy (sometimes called "uncertainty") is due to German physicist Werner Heisenberg

(1901–1976), stated in his "indeterminacy relations" (also called the "uncertainty principle"). This revolutionary notion insisted that there were pairs of properties of microscopic particles that could not both be known at the same time. These correlated properties allowed only a limited degree of specification. For instance, the more one knows about a particle's momentum, the less one can know about its position. If the momentum is specified precisely, then knowledge of position is lost. If position is specified precisely, then knowledge of momentum is likewise lost. As accuracy in the designation of one of the correlated properties is gained, accuracy about the other is diminished. So, the most that can be said is that a particle has a certain probability of being in a given position or possessing a certain momentum. So far this sounds only as if our abilities to measure these properties have some physical limits. While there are such limits, the implications of the indeterminacy relations are much more profound.

According to most thinkers in this area, Heisenberg has disclosed a fundamental limitation on what may be said about matter at its basic levels. No amount of technical advance will ever allow the "Heisenberg uncertainty" to be overcome. This leaves open the possibility that microscopic particles, usually said to include atoms and subatomic particles, do not even possess well-defined positions and momenta. If we designate very accurately, for instance, an electron's position, then, according to the majority interpretation of quantum mechanics, it does not even have a well-defined momentum. Conversely, if we specify its momentum, it has no single "position." Here we can see clearly the departure from classical physics, in which every object could, at least in theory, be measured to have these characteristics. Classically, every object has a particular position and a particular momentum. It makes no sense to think of a material object that does not have these properties, in traditional physics. But for Heisenberg and most of the rest of physicists in the twentieth century, atoms, electrons, and other phenomena of the micro realm are not classical particles. The atom is not a hard golf-ball-like nucleus (nor even composed of any such objects) orbited by smaller golf-ball-like electrons. None of these constituents exists in a classically understood fashion. Our ways of measuring, or looking at, these phenomena may force them to "take on" the appearances necessitated by our classical way of conceiving reality, but they cannot be said to possess these characteristics in themselves. The electron (or proton, neutron, photon, or even atom) cannot meaningfully be said to possess both a well-defined momentum and position.[4]

Likewise, in the two-slit experiment, the photon cannot meaningfully be said to have passed through one slit or the other. If we force the experimental apparatus to tell us which slit was used, then the experiment becomes a different experiment, and nature yields up the desired information, but only at the expense of some further information that we think also should be knowable. If we force an experimental apparatus to give a precise position for an electron, then we will get it, but only at the expense of thinking or speaking meaningfully about its momentum. The photon (or electron or atom) did not pass through one slit only, the electron (or photon or atom) does not have both specific position and momentum.

The assertions described in the previous paragraphs have sparked a good hundred or more serious philosophical difficulties. There is little agreement about how to talk about the physical meaning of the experiments and calculations. There is widespread agreement that the experimental results expose a world radically different from that presumed to exist by classical physics and by "common" sense. Many would take issue even with the way the results have been described above because I have used words such as "know" and "choose" in reference to obviously impersonal entities (even though I have used these characterizations negatively). These philosophical difficulties have engendered hundreds of books and articles aiming to solve the dilemmas apparent in the physics. Hundreds more have been written claiming to elucidate the meaning of these new scientific findings for issues beyond physics, from free will to pantheistic mysticism. Physicists usually scoff at these more fanciful "applications" of quantum physics, probably because they know that the new science is much better at telling what we do not know about subatomic particles than what we do know. Many physicists even scoff at any attempt to "interpret" quantum physics at all. The experimental results are clear enough mathematically, they will say, so why all the fuss about what is "really" going on in regions too small to observe directly? One thing is for sure, at least. Quantum mechanics yields fantastically accurate results about the behaviors of physical systems. The "quantum state" of a system at one time provides a precise basis from which to predict its quantum state later on. Our televisions and personal computers are testimony to this accuracy. The trillions upon trillions of electrons flowing through the circuitry of my computer right now behave very predictably, *en masse.* But this kind of predictability seems not to flow from any analogous predictability of any single component of the larger system. But the collective regularity causes many thinkers to hold that the indeterminacy of the single quantum is totally irrelevant to good science and even more irrelevant to grand philosophical questions about freedom or God or the paranormal or anything else.

The best lesson we can draw from more than seventy years of attempted interpretations and "applications" of quantum physics is to proceed with extreme caution. The dust is far from settled after the thought disturbance caused by twentieth-century atomic physics. Progress has been made, though, with regard to the philosophical puzzles, if for no other reason than many of the more fanciful readings of the theory have been shown to rely on no more than unsubstantiated assumptions. It seems we are asking better questions now, at least, and this is no mean accomplishment. So this chapter will proceed very cautiously, cognizant of how little we know with confidence about the individual residents of the micro-world. Thus we will treat three possible implications of quantum theory strictly hypothetically, exploring briefly what it would mean philosophically if nonlocality, observer-dependence, and randomness really are fundamental. If they are, as the majority interpretation of quantum theory suggests, then the end of certainty is clearly at hand. Then, and with a bit more confidence, we will turn to explore the degree to which quantum physics highlights a main contention of Peirce and of this book, that the ubiquity of signs and the inescapable sign-nature of our language form a powerful indicator of the end of certainty.

Where Is It?

Alfred North Whitehead was not thinking about quantum mechanics when he proposed that physical science often commits the fallacy of "simple location,"[5] but quantum physics provides perhaps the most notable example of what he meant. At the heart of classical physics is the idea that an object can be represented as existing at one place at a time. This "place" is usually depicted mathematically as a point in some coordinate system. But we learned in junior high school that the idea of a geometric point is an abstraction in that it takes up no space. So the spot on a two-dimensional coordinate plane corresponding to (1,1) cannot "hold" the object in question because this spot is not extended in space. Any "point" has a length, breadth, and height of zero. And the moment at which it is allegedly so located is not extended in time. The "present" or any single "moment" has a duration of zero. Our standard way of describing the motion of objects, then, utilizes mathematical idealizations, often presuming that these idealizations describe actual characteristics of the objects in question.

So it is very difficult to achieve accuracy and precision even with simple claims such as "3.7 seconds after impact with the bat, the baseball was 105.8 feet above the pitcher's mound." So we calculate the times and locations of idealizations like the "center of mass" of the baseball, an abstract concept that we are allowed to think of as a simple point. We pick out an instant at which to calculate the position of this point. For baseballs, the equations that describe these positions at these times yield the answers that we would expect—they (at least roughly) correspond to our physical experience. Neither the equations nor the baseball allow for it to be more than one place at one time. At any moment the baseball has a well-defined place (even if there are limits to the precision of our determinations of this place). Moreover, we can (apparently) speak sensibly about these qualities of the baseball independent of other entities in the universe. Its place at any given time can be thought of without our having to consider anything else. Its nature as a baseball does not seem to depend on any other event going on anywhere in the world.

For most of Western intellectual history, people thought that these common-sense qualities just ascribed to baseballs also applied to any real thing. Baseballs, planets, people, houses, churches, and books could all conceivably be located somewhere. They had absolute positions at any given time, whether we could actually know those positions or not. On the other hand, Hamlet, Captain Ahab, the square root of 2, love, and death were not "things" in the same sense. These could not be located on anyone's coordinate system. Hamlet cannot be found by zeroing in on his exact longitude and latitude. Hence (and for other reasons also) these items are denied the status of "thinghood." These things might not be denied the status of "real," as few deny the reality of love and death, but, at least since the late Middle Ages, the reality of these more abstract items was given only a derivative status. There cannot be, for instance, love without two or more individual "things" to exhibit that relationship. But there can be the persons without the love, so the "reality" of the relationship depends on the prior reality of the individuals who would be in it.[6]

So what sort of "thing" is a photon, or electron, or atom? Since these entities form the basis of the physical world, and since classical physics is quintessentially the science of reductionistic explanations, photons or electrons or atoms must have the characteristics of "things," understood on the analogy of the ball (or MSSO). The "thinghood" of these elementary particles seemed further confirmed by the discoveries of discreteness by Planck and Einstein. But the quantum physics version of the two-slit experiment throws a nasty curve at the practice of imagining these particles as something like little baseballs. The standard interpretation (named the "Copenhagen interpretation," after founder Niels Bohr's hometown) of quantum mechanics insists that these microscopic particles cannot be meaningfully said to have any simple location. This feature of quantum theory is known as "quantum nonlocality." It is extremely disturbing to those scientists who, like Einstein, wished to track the trajectory of any possible object in the universe just the way we would track a baseball.

When the single photon, or electron, or atom, passes through one slit or the other in the both-slits-open version of the experiment, the interference pattern appears on the screen. This means that something is going on besides a discrete particle following a path independent of all others. Its path seems to be definable only by considering other things that it might have done, or something else that it is doing at the same time in another place as it apparently passes through the slit. The interference pattern, remember, disappears when we succeed in detecting a unique trajectory for the particle. Most conclude, following the Copenhagen interpretation, that the particle does not have a unique trajectory, or a simple location at any given time, until our measurement forces it to take one on. At the moment of traversing the slit(s), the particle cannot have a simple location (like a baseball is presumed to have), or there would be no interference pattern. So where is it at this moment? Any answer to this question is controversial, which may be because the question itself is not well-formed. But the majority view (after Copenhagen, but supported by others, too) insists that there is some kind of "superposition of states" in which the particle is in neither place and at both. There seems to be no other decent explanation for the bizarre behavior of the quantum world. Or is there?

Now please let me take back most of what I just said in the last paragraph. Nonlocality is strange, weird, or "spooky" (as Einstein called it) only on the presumption that the photon or electron or atom is, in fact, a "thing" in the baseball-like way described above. If our concept of a real thing requires simple location (and other measurable properties), then nonlocality is tremendously bizarre. But is there any reason to presume that these inhabitants of the realm of the very small have these sought-after properties? The very statement made above that the photon somehow goes through both slits and neither assumes, in the definition of photon, simple location. Our very idea of thing, of which a photon is an example, presumes that it can be located like a baseball. But there seems to be no physical or logical requirement that photons (or any other sub-atomic entity) have these characteristics that we associate with objects of our everyday experience, MSSOs. Our current repertoire of thought pictures, by virtue of which we try to understand situations beyond our immediate experience, is not adequate for capturing the behavior of the very small. Maybe we will come to grips with quantum nonlocality through a new set of thought pictures, but this kind of cultural and linguistic evolution will take at least several generations.

A Roll of the Dice?

Among the most disconcerting aspects of quantum physics for Einstein was its insistence on a fundamental role for chance. Einstein expressed his distaste for chance by refusing to allow that God would "play dice with the universe." He was not alone in his resistance to this element of the theory. To admit chance, as we have seen above, is to admit the absence of some kind of explanation. For a thinker, especially a Nobel laureate physicist, this is tantamount to raising the white flag. What kind of truth-seeker would be content to foreclose all possible further investigation by declaring chance as the final word? For many thinkers, the invocation of chance as a fundamental descriptor of anything in nature is a failure of nerve. How presumptuous, they might say, to elevate one's inability to find an explanation to a universal principle denying even the existence of any explanation! These thinkers have a point, and the point is not lost on the defenders of the Copenhagen interpretation.

The issue between the defenders and resistors of chance bears some resemblance to the determinist/antideterminist debate that goes back to Democritus and Epicurus and which was revisited by Peirce in the nineteenth century. Determinists could always, with reason, argue that chance is only a concession to our limited knowledge and that further investigation will yield just the kind of explanations we want. On the other hand, anti-determinists can never decisively demonstrate that an explanation will never be found. Since a claim of chance, or randomness, is inherently a negative claim, it might always be proved wrong by the discovery of some phenomenon that provides the very explanation claimed to have been absent. If quantum mechanics demands that a radioactive atom decay at random, it claims the absence of any account of why the atom decays when it does. There is no way to know of any mechanism that causes the decay at that moment, rather than another. Whether or not there is actually some such mechanism is a different question and seems not to be answerable, at least not definitively. So determinists have taken heart in the limitation of human powers of observation and maintained their belief that the microscopic world is in fact rule-governed.

After many decades of ingenious experiments designed to give clues about the possible existence of these unknown rules or mechanisms (often called "hidden variables"), the issue between determinists and anti-determinists has often been recast into a question of the proper placing of the burden of proof. Experiment after experiment has continued to suggest that there are fundamental limits to what humans can ever observe about microscopic reality. We can only see the interference pattern, for example, when we are in a state of ignorance about which slit the atom passed through. This state of ignorance compels us to use probabilistic reasoning to predict only collective behavior (the interference pattern). Attempts to nail down individual behavior blind us to the collective behavior. Determining the momentum of an electron forbids our designation of its position, and vice-versa. This is different from a situation where more digging around may yield undiscovered truths, because the very act of observing one quantity makes impossible the determination of the other. Thus, it is argued, our ignorance in these areas cannot be overcome, so chance is here to stay. Because of the unanimous testimony of these experiments, many now feel that the burden of proof is on those who claim a deterministic underpinning to atomic behavior. The determinists are now cast in the light of ones who claim that the roulette wheel at the casino is rigged. Sure, they may say, the outcomes appear random, but the operator has made subtle, undetected manipulations in the wheel such that its results are predictable for him. If this is true, then the accuser is obliged to give the evidence for the fix, not merely state that it is possible.

Most interpreters have come to accept the random behavior of the microscopic world as a permanent feature, suggesting either that there is an objective randomness at work or that it is fruitless for us to speak of causes and explanations that we are forever forbidden from discovering. Put another way, whether atomic behavior is random from God's-eye-view or not, it always will be from our point of view, so it a waste of time to speculate about hidden variables. We must come to realize that statistical prediction (and "explanation") is the best we can do and live with its uncertainty. Asking what caused the atom to decay at this moment is searching for a kind of explanation that will not be found. Asking which slit the particle entered on its way to the interference pattern is asking a question that will not be answered and may not have an answer.

Part of the advance of human knowledge is the abandonment of questions determined not to be answerable. We no longer wonder about how many angels can dance on the head of a pin, the chemical makeup of the ether, or the nature of phlogiston. We do not ask about color of a number or the temperature of an electron. We no longer quiz ourselves about the actual location of the perfect circle or the address in heaven of righteousness. In quantum mechanics, leaving behind certain questions also seems advisable. It very well may be that we are interrogating nature with questions it cannot answer. Just as an innocent man cannot tell his questioners the whereabouts of the stolen loot, neither can our experiments reveal properties if they do not exist. If randomness is a real feature of the behavior of atomic nuclei, then our questions about what caused the atomic decay are poor questions. We have a long history of asking questions that do not have answers, of seeking explanations of types later agreed to be absent, so it is reasonable to suspect that the same thing is going on with regard to searches for hidden causes in apparently random systems. Just because baseballs and planets do not change without a physical cause (or we always explain their changes in terms of physical causes) does not mean that the smallest constituents of matter follow the same rules. Maybe we were wrong in expecting to find this kind of explanation for quantum objects. If so, then we have learned something very important in realizing it.

Not surprisingly, Peirce anticipated these difficulties by saying,

> Now it is one thing to infer from the laws of little things how great things, that consist of little things, will act; but it is quite a different thing to infer from the phenomena presented by great things how single things billions of times smaller will act. It is like inferring that because in any country one man in so many will commit suicide, therefore every individual, once in such a period of time, will make an attempt at suicide.[7]

This is precisely the same insight arrived at later by Niels Bohr, who came to see that many of the dilemmas of quantum mechanics arose from the attempt to apply macroscopic properties to microscopic objects.

Objective, Unbiased Observation

Many, though not all, of the problems unearthed by quantum physics are related to the decisive disturbance introduced into quantum systems by the act of observing them. In the two-slit experiment, the act of looking for one kind of result or the other affected what kind of result was obtained. If we look to see which slit was penetrated by the photon, we change the experiment irreversibly. This is usually interpreted as the measurement forcing the particle to assume one kind of value or another. If we don't know that individual value, then the interference pattern is present. Somehow it seems that our knowledge of the state of a system affects that system, such that it is no longer exactly the same system whose properties we initially set out to discover. This feature of quantum theory has stirred yet another tempest of controversy, most of which will be ignored here.

We should not, however, lose sight of the broader and ancient philosophical battle in which this is but a recent skirmish. Philosophers for a long time have realized that the act of observing makes a contribution to the knowledge of its object. We cannot form a pristinely unbiased picture of any universe outside our own minds. As we have already discussed, the information conveyed through electromagnetic radiation is only accessible to our eyes within a very narrow band of wavelengths. Our eyes, ears, and the rest of our senses are tuned to detect certain kinds of signals and not others. Therefore, what we describe as an experience of a world independent of our own individual sense apparatus is really a description of an encounter between that sense apparatus and some aspect of a world susceptible to detection by it. But the issue goes deeper than merely the particular competency of any individual's sense capacities.

As Kant showed so brilliantly, our minds also are "tuned" to experience only certain kinds of objects. In order for humans to have experiences at all, these (experiences) must be of a certain kind. At least sometimes (Kant said always), the objects of which we are conscious have the qualities they do because our minds superimpose those qualities. Thus, things appear as they do because our minds insist that certain qualities be present in anything that would be experienced. The shape of the world of our experience thus reflects the preexisting demands of the knowing mind, rather than some space-time structure in itself. So as we represent a world to ourselves, we do so as the painter who represents a scene on canvas—we paint what we are able to paint. As Nietzsche pointed out, the painter paints what he likes and likes precisely that which he is able to paint. If the human mind has no category for some object or event, then it will not be represented to the mind by the senses. Thus we realize that we can have no unbiased reading of the world. By looking at things in a certain way, I determine what sorts of things are experienced.

When our attention turns to the world of the atomic and subatomic, the impact of the observer on the observed becomes even more pronounced. We cannot observe a photon in exactly the same way that we can observe a golf ball. When an experimenter tries to locate the position of a photon, the photon is decisively affected. Its interaction with the detection device fundamentally alters the properties that we would hope to measure about it. Now something similar happens to the golf ball, but the effect is thought to be negligible. It is true that the light reflecting off of the golf ball, which allows us to see it and measure its position and velocity, affects the ball. But it does not affect it very much. So it seems an objective matter of fact whether or not it fell into the hole after 4 shots or 5. We can look at it without making it fall in. With microscopic reality this is not the case. Photons and atomic components are too small to measure without profoundly changing their characteristics. Hence we can never know what it is "really" doing when we are not looking. This observer influence is yet another source of our uncertainty about these objects (and may be the primary source, but this is another controversial topic).

A Long, Strange Trip

Golf balls and other middle-sized, stable, simple objects are composed of things that behave very differently from golf balls and other middle-sized, stable, simple objects. Yet classical physics (and philosophy and classical thought in general) presumed that analogous behaviors prevailed at any level of magnification. The disciplines of physics and philosophy of science are now quite confident that quantum mechanics has revealed a world radically different from the one pictured by classical concepts. We are far from confident, however, that our descriptions of the foundations of this world are even remotely accurate. We are still groping for a vocabulary with which to describe this new realm of experience. This is not an easy task, since we are being forced to reconsider some extremely well-established notions of what constitutes reality. Among other things, it seems we must abandon what was a bedrock presumption that any physically real object must be subject to causal laws (and thus causal explanations), has specific properties regardless of our "take" on them, and can be located unambiguously in space and time.

Golf balls do not move spontaneously from tee to hole; they do not fall in the hole because we looked at them; and they are never both in and out of the hole at the same time. Yet they are composed of entities that, analogously, seem to do all of these things. Hence our notion of what must be the case for any real thing must be drastically adjusted. This is not surprising, if we once again consider the reasons for the existence of language, and some of the history behind its development. Our language has developed in a context that required the naming of middle-sized, (apparently) simple, stable objects (MSSOs). Even today, if we say we understand something, we mean that we can form some sort of mental model or picture of it. These pictures are based on our experiences of the everyday world of middle-sized objects, and this is to be expected since any decent explanation must seek to account for the less familiar in terms of the more familiar. Everyone knows how a ball flies, but not everyone has a clear picture of atomic level reality. Quantum mechanics tells us that the microscopic world cannot be accurately pictured in terms of MSSOs. Predicates that seem to hold true of all middle-sized, stable, simple objects cannot be assumed to obtain in other realms. Middle-sized objects must be in one place or another, their characteristics hold whether or not someone is observing them, and they do not change or move without some force being exerted upon them. These statements seem to be true of golf balls and galaxies, of cheese and chimpanzees. It was once thought that any reality whatsoever must possess these kinds of qualities. Quantum physics seems to have changed all that. And this change is radical, because golf balls, galaxies, cheese, chimps, mice, and men are all composed of quantum level entities. Our traditional notions of existence and reality, of what a thing must be, are mistaken.

No Problem

None of the foregoing should be understood to imply that there are problems with quantum mechanics. Most practitioners are adamant that there are no serious problems with the physics. Our conundrums surface when we try to interpret the equations, when we infer from them something about what is "really" going on. That there should be difficulties at this point will be no surprise to persons aware of the issues raised in chapter 2. There are endemic problems in any attempt to get our signs and symbols to reflect unambiguously and accurately that to which they refer. These problems are exacerbated when the object picked out by the sign is radically different from the standard kinds of objects utilized in the development of the sign system in the first place. The mathematics behind quantum mechanics, usually referred to as the "formalism," is, like all thoughts and thought-schemes, composed of signs. These signs refer to objects and have meaning only by way of an interpretant (the equivalent, or more highly developed sign produced in the mind of the one receiving the "original" sign). Remember that a sign, in Peirce's system, refers to someone, for some person, in some respect or another.

The relevant notion here is that there is always some distance between a sign and the object to which it refers. This is true in normal, everyday speech, and much more so with quantum physics, where the formalism is highly abstract, and quite self-consciously does not attempt to refer directly to physical characteristics of individual objects. The quantum wavefunction refers to a quantum state and predicts future quantum states, but reference to a quantum state is not (directly) reference to a single object. The nature of the formalism itself imposes strict limits on the degree to which individual component parts can be specified (or referred to) at all. As a symbol system that seeks to describe certain characteristics of composite systems, quantum mechanics is magnificently successful. But it cannot pin down other characteristics, because it is not designed to do so. So as far as we humans are concerned, there will always be some level of "loose fit" between our equations and our world. The presence of this natural "wiggle room" may justify our seeing the world as a chancy, risky, open place, where our attempts to rationally circumscribe it are about on a par with "upholsterers and carpetlayers" measuring the surfaces they would cover with their specially woven fabrics. Our words and other symbols, all of which exist as signs, seek to "cover" our experience, to overlay it with order. Like the carpetlayer, tiny gaps in dark corners or closets will not destroy our efforts—unless these marginal imperfections occur in places where the fabric might begin to unravel, and that is the topic of the next chapter.

Notes

[1]Specifically, the quantity described in this way by Planck was "action," but his methods are easily seen to require that "quantization" also be applied to energy.

[2]"Planck's constant" is now one of the basic units in physics. Its value is approximately 6.625×10^{-27} erg-seconds.

[3]If the reader has already seen this experiment described a thousand times, he or she may feel free to skip to the next section.

[4]There are many excellent nontechnical or minimally technical books that describe in detail the experiments and further reasons to accept probability as fundamental. Two of the most accessible are John Gribbin's *In Search of Schrodinger's Cat* (New York: Bantam Books, 1984) and the more up-to-date David Lindley's *Where Does the Weirdness Go? Why Quantum Mechanics Is Strange But Not as Strange as You Think* (New York: Basic Books, 1996).

[5]*Science and the Modern World* (New York: Free Press, 1997) ch. 3.

[6]This is the ancient problem of nominalism vs. realism. This issue is fundamental to much of the discussion of this book. There will be a very brief treatment of this issue in chapter 8.

[7]CP 1.129.

For Further Reading

Austin, D. Brian. "Max Planck," "Niels Bohr," and "Werner Heisenberg," in *Great Thinkers of the Western World.* Edited by Ian MacGreal. San Francisco: HarperCollins, 1992.

Davies, Paul, ed. *The New Physics.* Cambridge: Cambridge University Press, 1989.

Gribbin, John. *In Search of Schrödinger's Cat.* New York: Bantam Books, 1984.

_____. *Schrödinger's Kittens and the Search for Reality: Solving the Quantum Mysteries.* Boston: Little, Brown, and Co., 1995.

Lindley, David. *Where Does the Weirdness Go? Why Quantum Mechanics Is Strange But Not as Strange as You Think.* New York: Basic Books, 1996.

Polkinghorne, John. *The Quantum World.* Princeton NJ: Princeton University Press, 1984.

Chapter 6

Habits upon Habits

Quantum mechanics has supplied a powerful, if not conclusive, confirmation of key elements of Peirce's worldview, specifically his ideas of chance and the limitations of our symbol systems. Thus it has helped paint a picture of a world that has much more in common with Peirce's notions than with those of his detractors. Peirce's worldview further suggests that from fundamental microscopic randomness patterns emerge, unpredictable in detail. Peirce conceives of these patterns (and our beliefs about them) as habits, and of the universe as "habit-taking." Furthermore, and to foreshadow a bit, we humans also create habits called "beliefs," which give shape to our farthest-reaching and most immediate convictions about how we will engage the future, a future cast in profound uncertainty. These beliefs, convictions, or habits are the maps that guide us into the fuzzy future, providing a framework within which we can handle even major surprises. They may even be seen as the "evidence of things hoped for." Does twentieth-century science give us any reason for accepting this broad outline of Peirce's, which sees the universe, including humans, as "habit-taking"? Is there any reason to believe, along with Peirce, that over uncertainty about the physical world extends beyond the realm of submicroscopic irrelevance? Chaos will say "yes."

Really Random Results?

A committed determinist (necessitarian) might greet the previous chapter with a yawn and a "so what?" Her confidence in determinism might take the following shape. "So, the microscopic world of the quantum is nonobjective, nonlocal, and nonpredictable. Does this really make any difference either to the practicing physicist or the weekend golfer? Even if the behavior of atomic level reality includes pure chance (which, by the way, could never be demonstrated), the physics of golf or bridges is not affected in the least. After all, when a golf ball and its billions of trillions of atoms are set in motion by a clubhead, the average behavior of that huge collection of atoms is predictable to any remotely desirable degree of certainty. The real world, where we all live, is enormously calculable, allowing Newtonian predictions to any imaginable useful degree of precision. So quantum mechanical indeterminacy and all-around strangeness have no impact on anything relevant to concrete human existence in the world of middle-sized objects, right?" Well, it's not that simple.

Thirty or forty years ago this attitude toward microscopic randomness was widespread and, given the data available at the time, perfectly justifiable. But today a number of converging movements in macroscopic physics cast serious doubt upon any strategy that would relegate even the most minuscule influences to realms of irrelevance. These sciences go by names such as "dynamical systems," "nonlinear dynamics," "far-from-equilibrium physics," "chaos theory," and more. In looking at the common features of these movements, we are taking quite a leap away from the concerns of the particle physicist. While quantum mechanics has often tried to catch the atom and its components in the act of doing whatever it is they do, these newer sciences are concerned primarily with the behavior of middle-sized collections of billions upon trillions of atoms and molecules. "Nonlinear dynamics" and related studies have shown the late twentieth-century world that nature is full of middle-sized systems (many of which we also call "objects," "entities" or "things") for which even the most minute influences can be momentous. These systems have several qualities in common that seem to coalesce in a way that permits such sublime sensitivity. The systems are complex, nonlinear, dynamic, and far-from-equilibrium. They are therefore highly unpredictable and often also very interesting, even remarkably creative. They are also highly volatile (even destructive and deadly), a trait that is a necessary correlate to the creativity. And these systems are all around us.

Insights gained from these new sciences have been applied to a dazzling variety of topics, from stock markets to heart rhythms, from population studies to weather. The universality of application is striking, causing many advocates of these methods to believe that they are working with newly discovered fundamental laws of nature.[1] These sciences are beginning to drive home a point analogous to one learned from quantum mechanics—the realities uncovered by these investigations are not adequately described with the existing vocabulary, the one built of models based on MSSOs. Like quantum mechanics, we need new words to account for the behaviors that emerge out of these processes. But as any new vocabulary must start with the old, we best begin by clarifying some of the terminology we have used to describe the kind of system under scrutiny. More specifically, our "thing" language, or words used to denote fundamental features of the real, will have to be extended to include "things" like "systems," "behaviors," or "patterns," which often have characteristics that are quite different from golf balls or rocks (or atoms or electrons). Shortcomings in vocabulary for these entities cause us to speak of systems "wanting" to go in a certain direction, or "choosing" one state or another, when we know that they do not have "free will" in the sense associated with persons.

Unstable and Off-Balance

Much of the groundbreaking work in the area of dynamical systems was done by Nobel laureate Ilya Prigogine of Brussels, Belgium, and much of the following discussion will rely on his explanations of his revolutionary work.[2] Prigogine has focused most of his research on chemical systems that are dynamic and "far-from-equilibrium." Put simply, this means that he works with systems that change constantly (unlike, for instance, crystals) and are highly organized and energetic. Thinking back to the example of a cup of hot tea, Prigogine's work is directed toward the tea when it is still very hot, rather than the tea after it has reached room temperature. Temperature is one measure of energy that can define a system as far from equilibrium, but there are others, such as motion or a variety of energies of chemical reaction, that serve to define a system as either near to or far from equilibrium. The tea after it has cooled to room temperature is near thermal equilibrium. This means that its molecules have reached the most probable distribution and average motions and that it has largely ceased to contribute energy to its surroundings. The average motion of the tea molecules has reached a stage comparable to that of the molecules in the room, and hence the tea no longer increases the energy of motion of the air molecules in its vicinity.

However, when the tea is still hot, its molecules behave very differently, and their energy is dissipated as it is transferred to the room, increasing room temperature ever so slightly. The behavior of this energetic tea turns out to be much more interesting than meets the eye and supplies an important example of extremely common far-from-equilibrium behavior. The process of convection, by which the hotter tea rises to the surface, cools, and then falls to make way for hotter liquid below, is a highly organized process, involving coordinated behavior of trillions of molecules. Thus their behavior is no longer random, or alternatively, they no longer are occupying the most probable state. These complex convection currents can be seen when a few drops of cream are added to the hot tea. The cream's contrasting color makes visible a very complex flow of rising, falling, and swirling regions of liquid. Each of these patterns is a kind of structure created when the fluid is far from equilibrium.

Now in what pertinent ways is this very simple example representative of other natural systems? According to Prigogine and others,[3] the processes of convection are representative of a basic tendency in nature toward "self-organization." Order, he says often, is generated "spontaneously" in some systems that are far from equilibrium. Simply by adding energy to one of these systems, order emerges, nonrandom structure occurs. The word "spontaneously" is a bit problematic[4] but not insofar as it suggests the unpredictability of new structures. Order does emerge in these systems, but most often we cannot tell which kind of order will emerge or what sort of change (fluctuation) will bring about the emergence of order. The kinds of systems he discusses can be clarified by analyzing Prigogine's following statement: "In far-from-equilibrium systems, there is no guarantee that fluctuations are damped."[5]

In systems near equilibrium, where stability reigns and there is no net contribution of energy to the environment outside the system, fluctuations are damped. The overall random motions of the molecules serve to bury the effect of any disturbance very quickly. The subsequent history of the system "forgets" the fluctuation. For instance, when my son throws a rock into the lake, the ripples soon die out, leaving no evidence of the plummeting projectile. The disturbance caused by the rock is absorbed by the (relatively) very stable average kinetic energy of the vast majority of lake water molecules.

If the system were far from equilibrium, however, the disturbance might not be so easily damped. The fluctuation might even be magnified or amplified to produce a twenty-foot wave that floods the city on the other shore. Now lakes can hardly be imagined to achieve this level of hydrodynamic instability, but many systems, both physical and chemical, do exist in an analogous kind of highly excitable state. The most readily apparent such fluid system is the atmosphere of earth, which can become so sensitive to minor disturbances that a microscopic disturbance in one hemisphere can instigate large-scale weather changes later in the opposite hemisphere. Obviously most of these tiny disturbances, flaps of butterfly wings, to cite an oft-repeated example, are damped. They are quickly forgotten by the large-scale system. But the complicated flows and swirls of an energetic region of atmosphere clearly can take one of these flutters and amplify it millions of times over. We will never be able to identify the offending Oriental butterfly by the time his own tornado rips through the American Midwest, but we know that influences even that small were crucial in the development of the storm.

Thus chaos theory has made a very notable contribution to the demise of modern science's dreams of certainty. The exquisite sensitivity of these systems highlights our inability to predict their behavior. Our best supercomputers will never be able to predict the detailed behavior of my cup of tea or if there will be a tornado in Kansas next year (unless the atmosphere of the earth ceases to be one of these sensitive systems). In the chemistry lab we cannot tell which pattern a far-from-equilibrium system will settle into when the temperature is increased one degree. The possible influences that may bring about new patterns are simply too numerous and too small for them all to be considered, and the interactions between the various component properties of these systems are vastly too complex to be calculated by specific analytical means (where the proper equation is used to reach a unique solution). As noted in chapter 3, whether these variations are instigated by fundamentally, or ontologically, causally random events cannot be demonstrated. Quantum mechanics may suggest that just such influences may be efficacious in these systems, or there may be other nonquantum sources of causal randomness. Even if there is not, brains like ours will remain stumped. Nature will always behave in ways that are surprising even to the most well-informed observer. This is because nature is full of precisely those kinds of systems that are able to magnify the minutiae, systems that are far from equilibrium and complex enough to show a macroscopic effect of even the smallest influence.

Prigogine speaks of this pattern-generation and its unpredictability in terms of "bifurcation points." If energy is added to one of these complex far-from-equilibrium systems, then the system approaches a critical point, one where its behavior can change into a more ordered form. But there may be different ordered behaviors that it can assume. The convection that begins as the fluid is heated, for example, may undertake a rotational flow in either a clockwise or counter-clockwise direction. Just prior to the point where the convectional flow is decided, some microscopic influence will cause it to turn in one direction or another. We know that convection must begin at this critical point, but we are powerless to tell which sort of structure or pattern it will be (unless our setup has been rigged to create a specific outcome). Nature is full of systems that behave in this unpredictable way at critical points.

By Their Own Bootstraps

One of the features that drives the creative instability of these systems is nonlinearity. Nonlinearity usually makes prediction extremely difficult. It makes clear analytic description very difficult. It is an aggravation for those of us who wish our numbers, words, and images to have clear referents. It makes many mathematical equations unsolvable. It also makes nature incredibly creative, destructive, and surprising. A nonlinear system is one that can take on radically new behaviors very quickly and unpredictably, often due to some kind of feedback loop, where the creation of a new pattern or structure itself allows for the creation of more of itself, thus rapidly accelerating its own production. This kind of feedback loop is well known in chemistry in the process of autocatalysis. Put simply, autocatalysis happens when the presence of a chemical helps in the creation (synthesis) of more of that chemical. So the more there is of it, the more of it is created. One can see how this can quickly produce massive amounts of the chemical in question.

Such nonlinearity is found in many systems that are far from equilibrium. In the hot cup of tea, convection currents encourage their own continuation, inducing neighboring molecules to join the caravan to the top of the cup. The fact that a hockey puck is moving helps it keep moving, because friction is less for a moving object than for a stationary one. Such processes are most common, however, at the level of living things. The population of rabbits does not grow at a calm, steady pace in lockstep with an increase in food and space because rabbits tend to make more rabbits, which in turn make more rabbits. With unlimited access to food and appropriate living space, rabbits would very quickly take over the world. But nonlinearity is perhaps best illustrated by behaviors familiar to every human adult. Individually, most persons are familiar with the experience of eating a big piece of cake because they were feeling down, only then to feel even worse for having given in to the temptation to eat cake, and then heading back to the cake to alleviate the worsened mood. Without proper constraints, this nonlinear "feedback loop" behavior becomes destructive very quickly. Of course the same pattern can be seen in creative, rather than destructive, behaviors. Positive moods tend to reinforce themselves, too, as known by anyone who has ever had the experience of "being on a roll" (which we might describe as a cascade of positive, creative actions).

Human collective behavior provides an even more obvious illustration. Many behaviors tend to spread like wildfire through a population, for no other reason than that they have spread through the population. People bought "Beanie Baby" toys because other people bought them. It is impossible to predict which "fad" items like these will "catch on" because of the nonlinearity of the process of gaining popularity and the zillions of products vying to be the lucky one. Gold is valuable because someone thought it was valuable, and its value is still dependent on such perceptions. Its value both causes and is caused by its being valued. And who could have predicted, before gold came to be so valued, that practically the entire population of the planet would treasure it so? No one, because there are plenty of other rare substances that might have caught the fancy of acquisitive humans, and gone on to play the role of supplying stability to a nation's monetary system (and other substances have so served). However, it might have been predicted that some such structure would emerge. It may be that a monetary system is the logical outcome of creatures like us trying to survive in community with each other. But the actual details of that system, the reasons why this pattern rather than another came to pass, seem to include inescapable reference to chance. As with other far-from-equilibrium systems (or structures, patterns, or entities), those that survive are only those that have adopted crucial stabilizing behaviors. Which complex behaviors cannot be told beforehand, but, like the convection currents, some pattern will form. The future is fuzzy for highly complex, energetic, nonlinear, feedback-looped, systems.

Remember chapter 4, where the existentialist interpretation of human "nature" bears more than a passing resemblance to the kinds of systems described above. For the existentialist, human existence never settles down because a person is always "making herself." The paradoxes of this way of speaking are paralleled in our discussion of systems that seem in some sense to cause themselves. In the development of a person, we say that our choices and plans (which most broadly are our convictions) define what we are. But this "definition" is always incomplete or falls short, because the me that is now is partly made up of the me that is not yet. If I am making myself, then I am never completely settled because I am changing any me that ever is. As long as I continue to exist, I will exhibit some patterns, but *which* pattern are not decided yet; never is it decided yet for the future, for that is the nature of future, existentially. I can never be a coincidence with myself, to use an image favored by Sartre. What lies at the root of any choice that I make in that lifelong process of defining who I am? What biochemical activity is taking place in the depths of my incredibly nonlinear brain that results in my helping the old lady across the street rather than stealing her purse? Was there a bifurcation point somewhere in the past that pushed me toward one state of being rather than another? Are those points happening now, as I create habits (far-from-equilibrium patterns) that will define my behavior (and my self) into the future? Can the macroscopic states of my collective self influence the paths followed by my microscopic component parts? These questions point to the heart of the mysteries of what it is to be a human person, and they can profitably be addressed by seeing nonlinearity in humans as something more than an illustration of nonlinearity in other systems. We are, among other things, the quintessential example of the very kind of physical system described by Prigogine and the others. The human organism is the most complex system that humankind has discovered in the universe. It is profoundly self-referential (with feedback loops at multiple levels), and therefore radically nonlinear. Thus it is also highly unpredictable, behaving in ways that we have come to regard as "free."

Whence the Novel Pattern?

Nonlinear behaviors are notoriously hard to pin down, to describe accurately, because they tend to change the very elements of the system that we would investigate in the process of seeking explanations. There is a sense in which these systems, whether convection currents or autocatalytic chemical reactions, "cause themselves." Now this is clearly an unfortunately sloppy use of language, but it is revealing. The convection current exists because there is a convection current. Chemical X is present because chemical X is present. There are rabbits because there are rabbits. Or, as an acquaintance of mine used to say, "I only drink when I'm drunk." So what starts each of these self-perpetuating patterns (a question presuming a more standard understanding of the word "cause")? This becomes a very hard question to answer, given the incredible sensitivity of the systems involved. Using Prigogine's language, each of these patterns was begun at some bifurcation point, a point at which an arbitrarily small influence inclined the far-from-equilibrium system toward one relatively stable structure rather than another. The influence could be so small that it might be best described as a clinamen or a quantum mechanical chance fluctuation (though remember that this speculation crosses the border from physics to philosophy). Chaotic systems are sensitive enough that they are affected at levels that appear forever inaccessible to standard human analytical modes of description. In other words, in looking for the ultimate microscopic causal explanation for certain behaviors or structures, we may be looking for explanations that we can never find, or even that do not exist (though this, too, can never be decisively shown).

Statistics Forever

The sciences of nonlinear unstable dynamical systems and structures have shown the world that statistical methods of prediction and explanation will be with us forever, or at least as long as human reason has anything like the shape that it now has. The only way we can predict behaviors of chaotic systems is statistically, with confident outcomes only for very large numbers of similar systems. It is not only with atoms and subatomic particles that our knowledge of single events or entities faces insuperable obstacles, but even our knowledge of a good percentage of middle-sized objects (and with practically all of the interesting middle-sized objects). Thus the future is fuzzy indeed, especially with regard to the energetic nonlinear systems that matter the most to us, human individuals and collectives. But we are coming to understand better the ways in which humans manifest the same kinds of behaviors evident at lower levels of physical organization. Prigogine expresses his most general understanding of the universe in this way, rejecting the presumptions that underlie the Newtonian worldview:

> Ours is a fluctuating, noisy, chaotic world more akin to what the Greek atomists imagined. . . . The clinamen [Epicurus] envisaged no longer belongs to a philosophical dream that is foreign to physics. It is the very expression of dynamical instability.[6]

Humans are systemically woven into this chaotically creative world. Like many inorganic systems, and like all living things, we too are (again, among other things) temporary dynamical structures, highly complex systems riddled with feedback loops of different kinds at different levels. As individuals and collectives, we are confidently predictable only probabilistically. Since we are nonlinear and complex, our futures are very fuzzy.

Engagement of that future in the authentic realization of its unsettledness requires a great deal of courage. The fact that the details of future events are irretrievably hidden from us does not mean that we have no idea of the course we would set toward that future. As an existential necessity (at least in the fallen and anxious condition in which we now live), we create potential action plans that will guide us through a future whose terrain remains clouded to our view. Understood in a Peircean sense, these action plans are nothing other than our beliefs, and our beliefs are nothing other than our action plans. In our capacity to form and to establish these behavior patterns, we once again reflect behaviors that, according to Peirce (and presumably Prigogine as well), are found throughout the universe. To understand how this might be so, we must examine Peirce's ideas regarding a notion much-neglected and (wrongly?) anathematized in the history of thought, the notion of "habit."

Humanity and the Habitual Cosmos

You may recall that philosopher David Hume had a hard time distinguishing our most important knowledge claims from habit. He argued that inductive reasoning (accumulating data from experience and generalizing from it to draw conclusions about the world) was suspect because it was nothing more than the habit of expecting the same things that happened before to happen again. For Hume, this implied a radical skepticism and a deep inadequacy at the base of all human attempts to know anything about the world. Charles Peirce agreed with a good deal of Hume's analysis, but rejected his denigration of the formation of habit as something less noble than "knowledge." If our alleged knowledge about the world is essentially habit, then so be it, but he argued that we should understand the nature of forming habits, and see that not only humans do it, but that all nature does it. The acquiring of habits is going on all around us, but most notably in those very same systems that Prigogine now describes as nonlinear and far from equilibrium. Other types of systems (structures or entities near equilibrium) have already established their habits. They are now no longer capable of significant growth and are much more predictable, since fluctuations in these extremely stable systems are uniformly damped (to combine terms from Peirce and Prigogine). This is why we (growing, habit-taking, far-from-equilibrium systems) will be unlikely to enjoy a fulfilling relationship with, for instance, a pet rock (a static, fully habituated, near equilibrium system). It does not respond noticeably to our touch (any effect is quickly damped) the way our lovers might (the effect just might be magnified and result in macroscopic consequences).

Thus habit is a key notion for Peirce, at the very heart of his understanding of the universe. Moreover, he sees all uniform, or law-like, behaviors to be the result of nature's habit-taking tendencies. But remember that they are not really laws for Peirce; laws are too restrictive, but habits may arise, change, and disappear. Patterns that we observe in nature have therefore grown into their current forms. For many patterns (or systems, or entities), the growth is practically over, as the natural end of a habit-taking tendency is a completely entrenched habit. For complicated, extremely sensitive systems, though, growth continues. Growth is nothing other than the acquisition of new habits (which may also involve the abandonment of old ones). Where does a new habit come from? It must be initiated from outside the current habit or pattern. In other words, it must occur by chance, at least from the explanatory perspective of the existing habit. To say that something happens by chance is to say that it is inexplicable under some kind of regularity (pattern) explanation scheme. So under Peirce's understanding of habit-taking, a new habit, by definition, must originate from outside the explanatory structure provided by the existing habit (the one that is altered or replaced by the new). So Epicurus' clinamen becomes part of the process by which the universe is able to grow new regularities. Something random must happen if there is really to be a *new* habit formed.

Peirce describes his views of the universality of habit-taking, and the role of chance, in this way:

> But any fundamental universal tendency ought to manifest itself in nature. Where shall we look for it? We could not expect to find it in such phenomena as gravitation where the evolution has so nearly approached its ultimate limit, that nothing even simulating irregularity can be found in it. But we must search for this generalizing tendency rather in such departments of nature where we find plasticity and evolution still at work. The most plastic of all things is the human mind, and next after that comes the organic world, the world of protoplasm. Now the generalizing tendency is the great law of mind, the law of association, the law of habit taking. We also find in all active protoplasm a tendency to take habits. Hence I was led to the hypothesis that the laws of the universe have been formed under a universal tendency of all things toward generalization and habit-taking.[7]

The work of Prigogine and the other "chaoticians" in the late twentieth century can be seen, as can the work of the pioneers of quantum mechanics earlier in the century, as a striking vindication of central elements of Peirce's vision. Quantum mechanics makes a strong case that chance must play a role in any description of the microscopic world, and thus suggests that Peirce's tychism, where he gives a key role in nature to real randomness, might just be right (at least from any perspective that humans as they are now constituted can ever hope to inhabit). Chaos theory describes a world in which the smallest of influences can induce a macroscopic system to adopt wholly new patterns of behavior (or structures). The convection currents in the cup of tea, then, can be seen as habits that were taken on by a sensitive system as the result of what can only be seen (at least from even an idealized human perspective) as a random fluctuation. Peirce would have been gratified to learn that sensitive systems like these are far more numerous than he could have known in his time.

Streams of Living Water

Perhaps the best illustration of the connections between human habit-taking and that of the rest of nature comes from Peirce himself. He asserts that "habit is by no means exclusively a mental fact. Empirically, we find that some plants take habits. The stream of water that wears a bed for itself is forming a habit."[8] This particularly valuable image of habit formation brings back memories of a stream table in ninth grade earth science class. The large, relatively flat, shallow table was filled with sand; one end was lifted to create the angle for water to flow down; and then a water source was turned on at the high end. We were amazed at the intricate and unpredictable channels that the flowing water would cut through the sandy surface. We were told that this table was a model of how rivers sliced their ways even through the hardest rock. Little did we suspect that we were also witnessing a potential lesson in everything from cosmology to psychology to epistemology to metaphysics. Peirce sees quite a universal lesson in the stream bed.

When the water first trickles across the sand (or the granite, for that matter), there are an immense number of possible paths open to it. No one can predict the path that will emerge in the future. Extremely small obstacles, even undetectable from our perspective, may cause the stream to move left rather than right. But once it has begun to carve its channel, it takes a much larger obstacle to divert it. It always is carving the path that defines itself. There is an interesting sense in which the stream makes itself. The stream is taking on a habit of digging this channel rather than another, and will continue in the habit, reinforcing it moment to moment, requiring a major disturbance to change the habit. In this example we see a number of elements of the systems described by Peirce and by Prigogine. Chance (tiny initial fluctuations), nonlinearity (it makes itself), and habit-taking (billions of trillions of molecules acting in concert) are illustrated by the stream. The Grand Canyon is one possible result.

The phenomena normally referred to as habits in humans have some of the same structure. In many cases we are unsure how they get started. Why does he tap his foot all the time? Why does she always put the right shoe on first? Why does one sibling love ketchup and the other hate it? More seriously, we might also ask why someone responds to stress by eating, smoking, or drinking. In all these behaviors a small beginning takes hold and digs a deeper channel in the psyche, often to the point where a major disruption is needed to change the pattern. Human habits are also like rivers in that some are wide and deep, while others are narrow and shallow. For most persons, giving up foot-tapping is probably easier than quitting smoking.

Peirce goes on to argue that all human behaviors, including language, belief, conviction, and the rest, are also profitably understood as habits. But unlike Hume, this does not count against the value of words, beliefs, or convictions. Habit-taking, on the contrary, can be seen as one of the most noble features of the universe, the very principle by which anything at all may come into existence and maintain that existence. The fact that humans exemplify this habit-taking tendency to the extreme is no indictment of human worth, but rather ennobles human beings as exemplars of creativity itself. Habit-taking affirms both stability and openness to novelty and growth.

A Fruitful Partnership

Chance and necessity, stability and growth, regularity and randomness, are all pairs of concepts that are usually portrayed as opponents. Such a portrayal is valid only if the pairs are referring to the same level of description, the same type of explanation. If the electron's energy level is said to jump randomly, then that does preclude the electron's obedience to law at some level. Its change cannot be caused by something and by nothing. Not even quantum mechanics requires a breach of this basic principle of logic. But random behavior at one level of description does not imply a lack of regularity at other levels. Specifically, individual atomic randomness does not imply a lack of regularity in the collective. A minuscule fluctuation at a bifurcation point in a teacup does not mean that all predictability in the system is lost. Once the convection pattern (habit) becomes established, then that structure will maintain stability, and hence predictability, for a time. Moreover, we know very confidently that the tea will be at room temperature in a couple of hours. Regularity and randomness work together in our universe to create a world that is stable enough for us to inhabit, but open enough for us to affect.

This means that our knowledge of this creative universe will always be somewhere between complete and worthless. But there are many persons who insist that we must know completely or we cannot know at all. They insist, in a parallel assertion, that nature is either random or regular. Such steadfastness in binary thinking belies the approach that we all take in negotiating a world about which we cannot be too sure. Persons act every minute on the basis of incomplete knowledge. I believe that if I leave the house in the car today, I will return in time to have dinner with my children. This means that I have a habit, ready to be applied when the opportunity arises, of getting out and about. That belief has direct practical bearing on the actions I take every day, but it is not certain. I am well aware that there are approximately 1,200 traffic fatalities in Tennessee every year and that I could be among that number this year. But my chances are pretty good of making it home at the end of the day, so I leave. The process by which I have formed this habit, this belief, is analogous to countless others. I make action plans based on beliefs, which are habits of thought, try them out in a world that is also in the midst of habit-taking behaviors, and see if they work. If they work, then I am that much more confident in my beliefs; those habits of thought are that much more engrained. When they don't, then there occurs an irritation, a doubt, a fluctuation in my far-from-equilibrium system that may just issue into the formation of a new pattern, a new habit of thought, a new belief.

We are creatures of regularity and sporting experimentation, further from equilibrium than most of the natural world with which we must interact, but carving our own channels in a world that is chancy itself. To suggest that there are random elements in the course of nature is not to suggest that there is no regularity, just as my announcement of my intentions for the future is not compromised by my admission that unforeseen circumstances might change that plan. You are regular but open, and so is the creative Creation. Even the theory of evolution, in which randomness plays such a fundamental role, cannot therefore be claimed to be entirely directionless. A casino can count on predictable profits even in complete ignorance about the outcome of the next hand of blackjack. I can count on my good friends to be faithful, even if tomorrow brings a temporary episode of negligence. A wise creator knows that the final product will be right, even if the path between here and there is indeterminate. The combination of chance and regularity, fruitfully intermeshed in a universe of habit-taking, will bring a "consummation devoutly to be wished" even if the eyes of finitude (or even infinitude?), gazing "through a glass darkly," cannot clearly resolve its image.

Notes

[1]Many of the natural systems that exhibit these kinds of behaviors are described in a very readable fashion by James Gleick in *Chaos: Making a New Science* (New York: Penguin Books, 1987). By the late 1990s practically every academic discipline had adapted principles from these new sciences to understand its own issues.

[2]My treatment will be woefully compressed. For minimally technical introductions to Prigogine's studies, see *Order Out of Chaos*, co-authored with Isabelle Stengers (New York: Bantam Books, 1984) and *The End of Certainty: Time, Chaos, and the New Laws of Nature* (New York: Free Press, 1997).

[3]Many persons have seized the opportunity to explore the further implications of Prigogine's work and of chaos studies more generally. Among the best of these are books by Arthur Peacocke: *Creation and the World of Science* (Oxford: Oxford University Press, 1979) and *Theology for a Scientific Age* (Minneapolis: Fortress Press, 1993).

[4]He may mean "in the absence of explicit goals" as part of the meaning of this term, which may suggest a conviction against all teleology. If so, then the term is probably too heavily loaded.

[5]Prigogine, *The End of Certainty*, 64.

[6]Ibid., 127.

[7]CP 7.515.

For Further Reading

Coveney, Peter, and Roger Highfield. *The Arrow of Time: A Voyage Through Science to Solve Time's Greatest Mystery.* New York: Fawcett Columbine, 1990.

Gleick, James. *Chaos: Making a New Science.* New York: Penguin Books, 1987.

Peacocke, Arthur. *Theology for a Scientific Age: Being and Becoming—Natural, Divine, and Human.* Enlarged Edition. Minneapolis: Fortress Press, 1993.

Prigogine, Ilya. *The End of Certainty: Time, Chaos, and the New Laws of Nature.* New York: Free Press, 1997.

Prigogine, Ilya, and Isabell Stengers. *Order Out of Chaos.* New York: Bantam Books, 1984.

Russell, Robert J., Nancey Murphy, and Arthur Peacocke, eds. *Chaos and Complexity: Scientific Perspectives on Divine Action.* Vatican City: Vatican Observatory Publications and Berkeley CA: The Center for Theology and the Natural Sciences, 1995.

Chapter 7

Evolution—
Chance, Life,
and Longshots

The most contentious issue between science and religion in the twentieth century has been the theory of evolution. Ever since the
publication of *The Origin of Species* by Charles Darwin in 1859, someone,
somewhere, in the Western world has been engaged in a debate regarding
its accuracy and its implications for the Christian faith. Though the extent
and the intensity of the debates have waxed and waned in the years since
1859, there has always been contention in some circles. But there have also
been many within the Christian church who saw in Darwin's ideas no
threat at all to their religious convictions. In the United States at the end of
the twentieth century, the debate has heated up again, to the extent that in
many ways one's position on the "evolution" question serves to identify on
which side of a cultural divide one resides. Yet contemporary science,
especially but not exclusively the biological sciences, cannot do without
evolutionary thinking. Notions employed by Darwin are everywhere in
the sciences, as specialists in many fields are finding, consistent with
Peirce's prognosis, that biological evolution is a specific instance of the
operation of principles that pervade all levels of natural development.
Evolution is habit-taking at its most complex, and it is a process in which
the role of chance cannot be ignored because chance is how new habits get
started; it is how new patterns and structures are initiated.

The Habit of Habit-Taking

Fans from both teams cheered wildly as the bat decisively struck the ball. The volume of the cheer doubled as the ball rolled between the shortstop and the third-baseman and the runner pounced gleefully, and safely, onto first base. This was the last game of the season, but the hit in question was not a series-winner, not a game-winner, not even a run batted in. But it was the triumphant moment of that little league season as that seven-year-old finally achieved a hit. His coaches, friends, and parents had kindly exhorted him all year with all sorts of helpful hints: "keep your eye on the ball," "watch it hit the bat," "don't step out of the box," "stride toward the pitcher," etc. None of it seemed to be getting through, as game after game saw him earnestly but unsuccessfully try to connect with that elusive ball.

Then, in that last game of a winless season, something clicked. For some reason, or maybe not, this time his swing was level, his weight shifted at just the right moment, his eyes stayed steadfastly trained on the pitch, his stride moved directly toward the pitcher's mound, and he hit that sharp and memorable single. His lights came on all at once, and he knew how to hit the baseball. Only after he had hit it did he begin to make cognitive sense of all that coaching. He happened upon the right combination of muscle movements, and then he knew how to hit the ball. From then on, in the postseason and in subsequent years, he could be counted on to be a hitter. That Saturday morning, a new habit was born, of largely random and fortunate circumstances, and because this habit was well-rewarded by a baseball-loving environment, it persists still. There is every chance that the young man will one day teach his own children to hit, further entrenching a family and cultural tradition (collective habit).

An amoeba happens to develop the ability to feed on lactose more efficiently than its neighboring amoebas. If it lives in a lactose-rich environment, then the habit persists, and any amoeba with this capability will flourish, and the habit very likely will be continued to successive generations of amoebas. Some habits, also called traits, extend from generation to generation, especially if they are beneficial within a given environment.

A trickle of water drips and then begins to make its way downward along the rock face, in apparently random motion. Very quickly it begins to carve a channel for itself along a specific course. As long as no obstacles impede the flow (that is, as long as the environment is conducive to its continuation), the habit persists. The channel becomes ever more entrenched as the water flows. The habit, originated as happenstance, is deepened, perhaps on its way to creating a Grand Canyon someday.

A giraffe-like creature just happens to be born with a slightly longer neck than most of its peers. Since food in their neighborhood is more abundant at greater heights, this fortunate creature is stronger and more robust than his counterparts, and thus more prolific. Hence he fathers a number of similarly endowed heirs. The long-neck habit becomes entrenched so long as the best and most plentiful food is elevated food.

It finally dawns on a struggling student how to do long division. After months of strife, this new and rather unnatural procedure is finally mastered. The steps are recorded in her memory, ready to be employed when the next opportunity arises. These mental patterns, somehow encoded through an enormously complex and poorly understood biochemical process, will persist as long as the environment is favorable, as long as her environment rewards long division (though with computers everywhere, the habit of long division is quickly fading for many persons).

All of these examples of habit-taking involve some degree of trial and error, some degree of chance (by which is meant, at least, a measure of independence between what starts the habit and the conditions that encourage its continuation). From some unapproachable realm a behavior is initiated in a system, and that behavior continues. Habits are born from outside existing habits, by definition. If we try to trace the origin of any habit, we will be led inevitably back to some limit of our powers of reconstruction. So we say that variations or fluctuations that lead to the development of new patterns are random. This is what Charles Darwin claimed was responsible for the origin of species. It is this assertion of Darwin's that is perhaps the most offensive to his detractors. For it seems to suggest that we, too, as complex persisting biochemical patterns, emerged purely by chance and therefore are ultimately a meaninglessly conscious, accidental perturbation in an otherwise blind and directionless universe. It is the purpose of this chapter to expose the deep deceptiveness and mistakenness of that inference. A Peircean reading of chance and evolution will help us undo this egregiously false and thoroughly dangerous understanding of humans and evolution.

Fat Chance

Chance was not a new concept during Darwin's day. Notions of chance events had been around for more than 2,000 years, the mathematical techniques for calculating probabilities had become well-established during the preceding hundred years, and Maxwell had even recently suggested that inaccessibly microscopic events might be able to affect the macroscopic state of a system. So did Darwin really suggest anything new with regard to the random? In a sense, he did, for Darwin opened the door for an understanding of chance as crucial in countless events of natural history. He did not view these microscopic chance events as inconsequential variations, easily damped by the sea of regularities that dominate nature, but as the source of raw material through which natural selection would move its winnowing fork.

Whether in a population of finches that survive because their long, thin beaks are able to dig deeply into trees for food, or the potato beetle that has now developed immunity to a popular insecticide, the advantageous trait emerged without any reference to the salutary effect. The variation (from short to long beak, or from non-immune to immune) is independent of its selective advantage (or disadvantage). The genetic code of the Galapagos finches did not "know" that a beak change was going to be needed, but when this trait emerged spontaneously (and maybe gradually), the environment quickly rewarded its possessor with a bounty of juicy, bark-dwelling bugs. Thus the collective "habit" of "long-beakedness" became established in that population in that environment. On a nearby island, on the other hand, where food was primarily found inside hard-shelled nuts, thick strong beaks emerged by analogous processes. As Darwin says,

> Mere chance, as we may call it, might cause one variety to differ in some character from its parents, and the offspring of this variety again to differ from its parent in the very same character and in a greater degree ...[1]

After the countless ages of earth's history, these chance variations will accumulate to produce quite divergent forms, each marvelously fitted to its environment. According to Darwin, nature appears to "bear the stamp of far higher workmanship"[2] than even the most impressive of human contrivances.

This explanation of the astonishing degree of "fit" between organisms and their environments came as quite a shock to many Christian thinkers in the nineteenth century. A very popular book of natural theology (a largely English movement that looked for evidences of the Creator in creation) attributed this remarkable correlation to the infinite wisdom of a loving God, specially designing creature and habitat for optimum success. William Paley's book, *Natural Theology*, catalogued scores of traits of humans and other animals that suited them so thoroughly for survival on this planet, that surely only God could have been responsible. Human eyes, for example, are so intricately adjusted for gathering information humans need to live that God must be an incredible engineer. Essentially, Darwin's findings suggested that Paley (and the legions persuaded by his type of natural theology) had it exactly backwards.[3]

On Darwin's reading of nature, species, including *Homo sapiens*, were developed in response to their environments, not the other way around. Many natural theologians seemed to presume that the complex organisms, reaching their apex in human beings, were conceived first, and then their habitats were constructed to suit them. Darwin's view, especially as developed by generations of followers, claims that the complex organisms that developed and survived did so according to their proficiency at surviving and reproducing in the environments dealt to them.

A nicely parallel debate occasionally pops up in twentieth-century arguments about God and design. When it was discovered that the ozone layer of the earth's atmosphere was precisely the right thickness to allow the development of life and to permit humans to exist here, some Christian believers latched on to this "fine-tuning" as evidence that God had made it this way. After all, if it varied even a little bit from the actual value, we would all freeze or fry. God's wisdom and compassionate foresight gave us just the right ozone thickness, according to this view. A Darwinian reading, though, asserts that humans were made for the ozone, not the ozone for humans. If that atmospheric layer were even a little different, then we would simply not exist. We exist on this planet because it supplies an environment to which our ancestors could successfully adapt. And adaptation begins with chance variation, according to Darwin.

If, by chance, you are born with a hypersensitivity to ultraviolet radiation, then chances are you will not survive long enough to reproduce offspring who would inherit that sensitivity. Thus the population is dominated by persons who are not so sensitive. Key to Darwin's under-standing of the variations is their independence from their effects. The variations will cause certain effects on those organisms that possess them, but the effect cannot bring about the cause. There is a real arrow of time in evolution. The level of ultraviolet radiation did not cause an organism to be born with a specific degree of tolerance. The first emergence in the chain of life of this tolerance happened by chance and was quickly entrenched in successive generations. The habit of ultraviolet tolerance began by chance, then it dug its channel deeply into living things on this particular planet. This also means that there is no particular reason, rela-tive to the outcome, why the unfortunate person is tragically born with a lethal hypersensitivity to something that the rest of do not even notice.

It must be noted, however, that Darwin did not feel that chance was fundamental in nature. He, like most thinkers of his era, believed that chance was invoked as an admission of our ignorance of specific causes. Darwin wrote,

> I have hitherto sometimes spoken as if the variations—so common and multiform with organic beings under domestication, and in a lesser degree with those under nature—were due to chance. This, of course, is a wholly incorrect expression, but it serves to acknowledge plainly our ignorance of the cause of each particular variation.[4]

So when Darwin spoke of chance variations from one generation to the next, he meant that (1) he could not identify the cause and that (2) the variation happened independently of its survival value (i.e., there is no teleological explanation). He asserts the unavailability of one kind of explanation (causal) and the absence of another kind (teleological). Hence variations are to be "explained" only statistically, in that some percentage of offspring will exhibit some degree of variation from their parents. In an analogous way, some percentage of gas molecules will deviate to some degree from the average kinetic energy of the collective of such molecules. What happens to any individual organism, or molecule, is beyond our ability to explain or predict. Maxwell's molecular motions and Darwin's hereditary variations presumably had causes, but the prospects of our ever uncovering them were vanishingly small. Not until the philosophy of Peirce and then the advent of quantum mechanics did anyone seriously suggest that uncaused events might actually happen, or, to put it a different way, that a key sort of randomness might be fundamental (or ontological).

Not So Strange Bedfellows

Politics makes strange bedfellows, and when evolution turns political, it brings together apparently unlikely pairs. There is widespread agreement among interpreters of evolution (including those who deny that it happens) that it affirms the independence of variation and effect, but less agreement on whether these variations should be seen as causally random. But even the weaker claim, that variations are undirected, is thought by many to have cosmic significance. Many twentieth-century writers, including unlikely allies such as biologist Richard Dawkins and creationist Philip Johnson, agree that evolution's insistence on undirected variations implies a universe without purpose or meaning.

This alleged implication of evolution is famously delivered by Nobel laureate Jacques Monod in his 1970 book *Chance and Necessity*. In a telling mixed metaphor, Monod affirms that "chance *alone* is at the source of every innovation, of all creation in the biosphere. Pure chance, absolutely free but blind, at the very root of the stupendous edifice of evolution."[5] Chance's fundamental role in evolution leads Monod to the following melancholy assessment of humans' (though he does not use such inclusive language) hopes of any transcendent meaning:

> Now does he at last realize that, like a gypsy, he lives on the boundary of alien world. A world that is deaf to his music, just as indifferent to his hopes as it is to his suffering or his crimes.[6]

Monod calls upon all those who possess "some element of culture, a little intelligence"[7] to share his profoundly anti-religious understanding of the cosmos, and apparently to affirm with him the concluding sentiment of his widely read book:

> The ancient covenant is in pieces: man knows at last that he is alone in the universe's unfeeling immensity, out of which he emerged only by chance. His destiny is nowhere spelled out, nor is his duty. The kingdom above or the darkness below; it is for him to choose.[8]

At least in broad outline, Monod's interpretation of evolution is shared by a wide array of well-known discussants in today's public conversation about evolution. Atheists such as Richard Dawkins, William Provine, and the late Carl Sagan all see in evolution's reliance on chance-endowed natural processes reason to dismiss religion's claims that the cosmos exists and develops for some grand purpose. The "scientific" creationists, the slightly less radical "intelligent design" proponents, and other anti-evolution Christians see the same thing. This is why atheist William Provine is a frequent participant in creation-evolution debates sponsored by Christian organizations—both they and he operate from an agenda that insists on the incompatibility of evolution and Christianity. Extreme factions among both atheists and Christians are vigorously and loudly opposed to any mediating position, such as theistic evolution. The two extremes, atheistic evolutionists and anti-evolution Christians, are united against a common enemy, even while they are bitterly opposed to one another. The black and white have joined forces against the gray.

These two groups do have the advantage of understanding each others' language. Members of both camps share a strong desire to escape the onslaught of the end of certainty that threatens to bring religion and science together in a humble admission of finitude and near ignorance in the face of the incredible mysteries of the complicated and creative cosmos. Two diametrically opposed fundamentalisms are defending their common methodology from the perceived threat of an alleged postmodern intellectual vacuum. Both camps share an enormous confidence that their words are accurately, even literally, descriptive of some reality beyond their own minds and that their beliefs are somehow immune to the limitations of linguistic expression discussed in chapter 2. Many scientifically inspired atheists seem to reflect Monod's worldview, communicating an attitude that says "The data said it, I believe it, and that settles it; and if you disagree, then you're stupid." On the other side, anti-evolution Christians in this kind of debate have been heard to utter the remarkably similar dictum "God said it, I believe it, and that settles it; and if you disagree, then you are condemned to hell." In a culture that prefers sensational controversy and bumper-sticker philosophy to rational and respectful discourse, the "debates" between these two perspectives draw great crowds. There is a strong sense in which advocates of both of these positions speak the same language. It is the language of a confident Cartesian worldview, a view that sees objective certainty as obtainable, if not already attained.

Their extreme confidence that their words and equations literally and comprehensively convey fixed truths about the universe, born more of a deadly blend of wishful thinking and fear of the fuzzy than of a careful analysis of the ways that words and other symbols actually refer to their objects, is a lasting legacy of modernity's Cartesian dreams of certainty. A Peircean perspective, one laden with faith directed toward an unpredictable future, would hope that it is the last legacy.

Plan for the Unexpected

Of course, the operation of chance in nature (whether fundamental or merely subjective) and the uncertainty and indeterminacy it brings do not really imply either the impossibility of knowledge or cosmic purposelessness. Leading religion/science thinker Arthur Peacocke, for example, argues that Monod has simply committed a logical *non-sequitir* in supposing that microscopic randomness means cosmic blindness and deafness. Peacocke thinks there is no reason why molecular randomness "has to be raised to the level of a metaphysical principle interpreting the universe."[9] Monod's elevation of randomness to this level resembles what logic teachers call the fallacy of composition, where qualities of the part are automatically presumed to describe the whole they comprise. Just because every brick in the house is able to be lifted by one human, it does not follow that the house made of these bricks can be so lifted. Just because one coin toss is unpredictable, it does not follow that the long run of tosses is not predictable. Just because mutations are random, it does not follow that the global system of which they are a part is random. In general, then, the presence of micro-level chance does not mean that the macro-level processes they comprise are either inaccessible to our reasoning powers or that they are directionless or meaningless.

For example, each spin of the roulette wheel yields a random result (from any fair human perspective), yet the profits for the casino owner at the end of the month are all but assured. The wheel, in fact, has been purposefully created or designed to produce just such random outcomes. A random five-minute run of luck (good or bad) cannot be extrapolated to a conclusion that the month's collective results are random. Similarly, randomness in atoms or in genetic variations cannot be a reason to presume that the container of gas or the population of organisms also defies rational explanation or long-term predictability (at some appropriate level of generality). The large-scale purpose (such as casino profits or increasing biological complexity) might be accomplished by very many different distinct routes. The casino owner does not care if Saturday's closing hour is weak, or about any given hour, so long as the profits for the month meet expectations.[10]

By analogy, evolutionary "goals" might very well be reached by any number of different paths to those goals. There are innumerable trails to the top of any given mountain. The temperature of a container of gas might be realized by a very large number of possible distinct distributions of energies of specific molecules. As offensive as it sounds to some who have inherited a Platonic-Cartesian type of necessitarianism or hyperrationalism, specific genetic variations, even those leading to the emergence of *Homo sapiens*, might also be strictly irrelevant to the accomplishment of a Creator's long-term purposes. It is clearly conceivable that a Creator might wish to create a universe where a prodigious variety of highly complex, self-aware (and thus nonlinear), growing, learning, entities might emerge. Our universe seems to be shot through with the potential for the emergence of just these kinds of creatures. There is no need for them to have looked just like us. The kinds of complex systems engendered by the kind of world in which we live take on a great many forms, even on this tiny planet. There may well be other planets harboring creatures also made in the image of God, and they may be legitimately described in this way even if they bear little outward resemblance to ourselves.

The history of life on our own planet suggests that accidents played a major role in shaping the forms that developed. The fact that we humans are bipedal, have the kind of visual apparatus we do, think the way we do, and have the features we do, might easily have been otherwise. Any of thousands of crucial genetic variations along the way to *Homo sapiens* might not have happened, and thus we might have turned out drastically different than we actually did. But even if we are, in part, the product of a million accumulated accidents (random variations), this does not mean that we are not part of a marvelous plan. The import of the "accidental" emergence of biological form can be illustrated by reflection on the "accidents" that lie in the prehistory of any individual human being.

Child of Chance

The realization that I might not have happened struck me during late childhood. My, and our, radical contingency hit home one day as my mother took me on a nostalgic journey through her high school yearbook. She happened upon a photo of an old boyfriend she had dated before she met and married my father. "If I had married him," she said, "he would have been your father." I was immediately and profoundly impressed by the literal falseness of her passing remark. "If she had married that other guy," I thought, "then I would never have existed at all!" This was most decidedly a disturbing prospect. My genetic information was specifically brought into a unique combination by the union of Mom and Dad, not Mom and the lost boyfriend. Moreover, the environment that impinged upon the products of that genetic code was inviolably pervaded by my experiences of Mom and Dad. "Mom and the other guy" would have produced an entirely different person, not me at all. If Dad had chosen a different college, had not attended that town-and-gown mixer where he met Mom, not decided to ask her out, etc., etc., then there simply would not have been a "me" in the first place. This is only the beginning of the story of life and contingency.

We know that the human sperm cell that succeeds in fertilizing the egg cell is one of millions vying for that chance. A different sperm cell creates a different person. The egg cell's own genetic information represents one out of more than 8 million possible combinations the mother might have produced (just based on possible arrangements of the 23 chromosomes in the cell). With each of the father's sperm having a similar variability, any human coupling might produce more than 70 trillion different possible offspring. According to French researcher Remy Lestienne, this number, which is more than 10,000 times the population of the entire planet, "is the minimum number of possible variants for the genetic endowment of children of the same mother and father."[11] He further explains other sources of variation in the production of the germ cells themselves (sperm and egg) and concludes that "a single individual has the power to engender on the order of at least 10200 different spermatozoa or eggs."[12] This is vastly more than can ever be realized. Furthermore, "[i]f we add the chance social events that preside over the encounter of a given father and mother, we are, as are our children, truly the children of chance."[13]

In the astronomical unlikelihood of any single human individual, we see an analogy for the unlikelihood of the emergence of any specific species itself. The variations that give rise to a new variety (or species, or whatever) of plant or animal come from the massive reshuffling of genetic information described above. The odds against the emergence of *Homo sapiens* are incalculably large. The odds against any individual member of the group *Homo sapiens* are therefore even larger. One might be tempted, on this Darwinian account of the chance origins of existing life forms on earth, to conclude that randomness is the whole story and that religious talk of cosmic purpose, of creation and redemption, is summarily ruled nonsensical. Such a conclusion, though, is not warranted.

Peirce and the Human Habit

We may not be able to predict the eye-color, or facial features, or musical or mathematical aptitude of a coming child with complete accuracy, but we are quite confident that he or she will be human. There are, in other words, a great number of patterns we can count on in the development of the embryo and the person. We do not know if our children will be geniuses or not, but they will be human children, bearing some resemblance to their parents, so randomness is not the only word. There is colossal possibility for variants, but only within regular constraints. These constraints are the persistent habits of the human genome. The "human habit" in nature has been extraordinarily successful and, like the stream carving its bed in rock, has entrenched itself deeply into the biosphere of the planet. It will continue, like all habits, until an obstacle forces a reorientation or until at its tractable cutting edge a drift (a *clinamen*?) begins a new channel. The human habit, like the rest, is more changeable at its edges than at its core, so there is continuity and variability.

In every successful human conception, gestation, and birth something very interesting is initiated. Given the massive complexity of this genetic habit in nature (humans), something intriguing, *prima facie* valuable, will come to be, but something only partly determinable by the nature and will of its procreators. Contemporary science, since Darwin, suggests that much the same can be said of the beginnings of the expectant universe. Given the habit-taking nature of the developing, historical cosmos, something very interesting is bound to emerge. Given the available raw materials and pattern-generating tendencies of that material in far-from-equilibrium conditions, some fascinating habit will be instigated. The kind of universe exposed by recent science is a universe that inevitably creates pockets of order, using up available energy for the creation of complex persisting patterns.

Could this not be a description of a kind of purpose in the universe, a purpose realized through a remarkably pregnant cooperation between chance and pattern, between randomness and regularity? A Peircean habit-taking universe is deeply teleological (goal-oriented); it is going somewhere, though (and this is crucial) no one knows precisely where. Thus I, or you, or any individual might not have happened, but each of us is a part of a cosmos where creativity is a fundamental feature, creativity in the form of habit-taking that results in new and increasingly complex forms. We did not have to be specifically foreordained in order to be part of a meaningful, directional, project. *Homo sapiens per se* might not have happened, but we nevertheless are part of a plan, once as a vague possibility, now as a detailed actuality, if we interpret evolution theistically. In other words, it is conceivable that a theistic God's intention in the creation and sustenance of our universe did not specifically include human beings as they now exist, but did, perhaps, include the emergence of highly non-linear, self-referential complex entities with the potential to glorify and please their Creator. Entities of this sort will be very interesting and markedly unpredictable, and it would be very difficult to find a reason not to employ the word "free" to describe their behavior. But they need not have four limbs, upright gait, distributed-processing brains with their characteristic thought patterns, endoskeletons, or any other accidental feature of modern humans.

Creatures in the image of God could have turned out in an indefinite number of ways, but, on the analogy of a parent, their creator will love them however they look. Their value is not dependent on the preexistence of a detailed blueprint. Their worth is not tied to their playing out a precise script. The chancy, risky process that creates a new habit in the universe, whether a new species or a new organism, a new behavior in an organism, or a new cultural practice, is fraught with real unpredictability, and this is why they matter at all (a central theme of part three of the book). Our risky kind of world is the only one where covenant and devotion can get any traction at all, because foregone conclusions, like widely accepted mathematical formulas, do not inspire or require personal commitment and conviction. A spouse or a child, because they and their reception in the world are unpredictable and mysterious, enjoin faith. The bride of Christ, or the children of God, stand in this kind of relationship to their bridegroom, their creator, in a risky world that gives substance to commitment. If marriage or parenthood were a foregone conclusion, then the word "promise" would never have entered our vocabulary. Only a fuzzy future, with real options and attendant risks, gives real weight to promise, trust, and faith.

Knowing All That Can Be Known

Two very basic philosophical questions for the ages are related to each other: "Why is there something rather than nothing?" and "Why this kind of something?" If the contemporary scientific world picture is closing in on truth, then the second question can be posed more specifically: "Why this risky habit-taking world?" The Christian answer must lie in the will of God. One possible answer might assume the following trajectory: "A world like ours, driven by the creative, evolutionary interplay of chance and pattern is the only kind of world where covenant and devotion can occupy center stage, where reconciliation of brokenness might sensibly be played out in faith." It makes theistic sense to suggest that the cosmos has this risky unpredictability (chance, uncertainty), this creative ability to engender new habits (regularity, pattern) because the theistic God (who is a personal God) created it this way.

To say that the emergence of humans as we now exist might not have happened, might, however, raise some difficulties in our conception of God. We know, for instance, that from our perspective the possibilities for what kind of life would emerge on earth were vast, but we do not know if this contingency is fundamental. In other words, were there numerous real possibilities even from God's point of view? If God is all-knowing from the moment of creation, then was there ever a possibility that any other kind of creature would have taken our place? A pricklier question may not exist in the history of philosophical theology. Contributions to this and related debates have spawned some of the most contentious and technical philosophical debate in the last 700 years, a debate we do not have the luxury of entering here. It must be noted that a growing number of theologians are willing to entertain the idea that not even God can know ahead of time what random or free events will actually occur.[14] According to this line of reasoning, such lack of knowledge is not an indictment of omniscience because God is still said to know all things that can be known. But many things cannot be known as actual because they are not actual yet. For example, the exact genetic structure of *Homo sapiens*, or what I will have for breakfast on my seventieth birthday, could not have been foreknown because these events did not exist to be known (before they actually happened).[15]

Though this account of omniscience strikes me as an overly anthropomorphic (humanlike) conception, it does have the advantage of making sense of the idea of a covenant between God and the people of God. For God, understood in this way, takes risks. God would not know in advance exactly what would emerge from the magnificently fertile universe of habit-taking that God had made. But God would know that something free and worthwhile, something also (like its creator) able to experience risk and loss, would surely happen. These complex, energetic, self-referential organic habits might, in fact, even choose to reject the nurture of their creator, but that is the chance love takes. The child may rebel against his parents, the randomizing creativity of genetic shuffling may occasionally produce agonizingly lethal congenital defects. The very wonders of human intellect and creativity might be turned toward genocide, but these are the chances love takes.

God, Chance, and Poetry

One of the sources of resistance to this view of God and the world is our rich poetic tradition that attributes eternal significance to those things that matter the most to us. Events and entities that impact us deeply are often attributed to destiny or to the eternal plan of God. For instance, devoted husbands and wives often speak of themselves as "soulmates," scripted from the foundations of time to find each other. Unmarried persons might look for Mr. or Ms. Right, as if there were but one individual in the world foreordained to be each's partner. When a divine mission burns deep within our bones, we might affirm with Jeremiah that God knew us and called us even before we began to take shape in our mothers' wombs (Jer 1:5). From the viewpoint that sees the world as fundamentally risky, these are all marvelous poetic celebration of spiritual springs of meaning that bring us nearer to communion with the God of our covenant. But for much of the Platonic West, profoundly uncomfortable with contingency, these poetic claims have been imbued with a kind of literality that the symbols will not bear. Our deep desire to escape chance and fuzziness, and their endemic uncertainty, has led us to try to squeeze the messy and malleable world of living and unpredictable things into the molds of rigid conceptual schemes where everything (at least everything of importance) happens by some sort of inexorable necessity (whether mathematical, divine, or both).

The world described by twentieth-century science confronts us with radical contingency, fuzziness, and chance that will not step aside. From atoms to gases to spouses to children, contingency reigns. There are millions of women I might have married, and billions upon trillions of possible different children we might have produced. Yet I have written poetry about the eternal compatibility and inestimable value of the family that actually came to be. That the persons in my family could have been countless others detracts not one iota from the meaning and fulfillment that they bring to me and to each other. As hard as it is to imagine a world where these particular, specific, individual children of mine do not exist, such a world was a distinct possibility some twenty years ago. As hard as it is to imagine my life without my specific, individual, particular wife, such a life could easily have happened. As hard as it is to imagine a planet where humans just like us never emerged, such a planet was a real possibility just a short few million years ago.

At least this is the picture of the world painted by the growing consensus in contemporary scientific thought. It is a world that is perfect for the development of faith, especially when seen from the perspective of increasingly complex episodes of habit-taking. It is a world where commitments mean something because they will press against the unexpected; they will grow as the world grows. They will help to give shape to the malleable future as the committed respond to God's call to sacrifice and redemption. Only the end of certainty beckons faith, a faith that is more than empty words. As Peirce shows us, words that do not set a trajectory toward an open future are the emptiest of all.

Notes

[1] *Origin of Species* (New York: P. F. Collier & Son, 1937) 115.

[2] Ibid., 91.

[3] Darwin was not the first to suggest that natural theology had it backwards. David Hume, in his *Dialogues Concerning Natural Religion,* argued that adaptability could easily give the impression of special design.

[4] *Origin of Species,* 138.

[5] *Chance and Necessity,* trans. Austryn Wainhouse (New York: Vintage Books, 1972) 112.

[6] Ibid., 172-73.

[7] Ibid., 171.

[8] Ibid., 180.

[9] *Creation and the World of Science* (Oxford: Clarendon Press, 1979) 94.

[10] David Bartholomew, in his 1984 work *God of Chance* (London: SCM, 1984), illustrates many more large-scale purposeful endeavors that incorporate randomizing strategies within them. Throughout this book Bartholomew argues for the compatibility of chance and purpose, and draws theological conclusions in accord with many of my own.

[11] *The Creative Power of Chance,* trans. E. C. Neher (Urbana and Chicago: University of Illinois Press, 1998) 54.

[12] Ibid., 85.

[13] Ibid.

[14] See any number of process theologians, along with Richard Swinburne, *The Coherence of Theism* (Oxford: Clarendon Press, 1977), and more recently from the evangelical tradition John Sanders, *The God Who Risks: A Theology of Providence* (Downers Grove IL: Intervarsity Press, 1998). This perspective on omniscience also received favorable treatment by Anthony Kenny, John Lucas, Arthur Peacocke, David Bartholomew, and many others.

[15] For more on probability and God's knowledge and providence, see my article "Randomness, Omniscience, and Divine Action" in Jitse van der Meer, ed., *Facets of Faith and Science,* vol. 4 (New York: University Press of America, 1997).

For Further Reading

Austin, D. Brian. "Randomness, Omniscience, and Divine Action." In *Facets of Faith and Science.* Vol. 4. Edited by Jitse Van Der Meer. New York: University Press of America, 1997.

Bartholomew, David J. *God of Chance.* London: SCM Press, 1984.

Kitcher, Philip. *Abusing Science: The Case Against Creationism.* Cambridge MA: MIT Press, 1982.

Lestienne, Remy. *The Creative Power of Chance.* Translated by F. C. Neher. Urbana and Chicago: University of Illinois Press, 1998.

Peacocke, Arthur. *Creation and the World of Science.* Oxford: Clarendon Press, 1979.

Polkinghorne, John. *Science and Providence: God's Interaction with the World.* London: The Longdunn Press Ltd., 1993.

Ratzsch, Del. *The Battle of Beginnings: Why Neither Side Is Winning the Creation-Evolution Debate.* Downers Grove IL: Intervarsity Press, 1996.

Sanders, John. *The God Who Risks: A Theology of Providence.* Downers Grove IL: Intervarsity Press, 1998.

Chapter 8

Of Machines
and Apes

Generally speaking, people do not like being compared to apes or to machines. Apes are comical or foolish, machines are, well, mechanical. Something about humans is altogether more interesting, nobler, and freer than these poor contenders. Yet human discovery and invention in the twentieth century seem to be exposing more and more similarities between humans and apes and computers. The human affinity with other higher primates proposed by Darwinian theory was perhaps even more offensive than the notion that our shapes emerged by chance. Yet the overwhelming accumulation of scientific data confirms our profound kinship and likeness to our apish friends. Advances in genetics continue to affirm Darwin's insights into human ancestry, as proficiency in the analysis of the molecular components of heredity grows almost daily. It is hard to believe that the science of genetics has grown so greatly since the relatively recent (1950s) discovery of the shape and function of the DNA molecule in living things, to the point where we can confidently claim that human and chimpanzee DNA is more than 98% identical. This booming area of science will likely provide some of the most strident challenges to persons of religious conviction into the twenty-first century, because we are learning more and more of the details of how, and to what extent, our DNA determines what sort of creatures we are.

At the same time, and not unrelatedly, cognitive science and artificial intelligence (AI) continue to demonstrate how behaviors once thought possible only for humans can be observed in human-made machines. The widespread use of computers has made computer analogies almost second nature in our discussion of everything from bacteria to persons. For example, DNA, the molecule of life, is said to "encode" the properties that give shape to what we are. This almost universally applied analogy is drawn from the computer sciences, a movement that saw its great awakening about the same time as did molecular genetics. Hence it is often remarked that DNA is like a computer program that generates as output a particular organism.

Traditional views of human nature, particularly those associated with a Christian worldview, are thus being challenged by an understanding that likens us (and all living things) to very complicated machines, running out an interactive DNA program. Plato's dualistic understanding of humans as body and soul, imported to a stubborn place in Christian theology by Augustine, and made more intransigent by Descartes' wedding of it to a modern scientific worldview, is being whittled away. As many doctrines important to Christianity seem to depend upon some version of this dualism, many believers feel quite threatened by the apparent lessons we are learning about ourselves from genetics and from artificial intelligence. Moreover, these fields promise only greater and greater advance into the next century.

A number of biologists and AI leaders are convinced that humans have been shown to be nothing but moist information-processors, imperfect and therefore unpredictable computational engines whose structure, flaws and all, will be uncovered more and more as our understanding increases. They argue that our convictions, our ethics, and our "spirituality" are nothing more than genetically or culturally imposed behaviors, referring to nothing beyond themselves because there is nothing beyond. As was the case with the anti-theistic evolutionists, these conclusions against transcendence, against meaning and value, are not warranted by the data claimed in their support. Once again Peirce can help us to see that machine analogies do not tell the whole story. Arguments alleging to strip humans of any divinely installed dignity by pointing out their close likeness to computers or to apes, paradoxically, often rely on the very kind of dualism that these new sciences are helping to explode.

A Baby Robot

In a laboratory at the Massachusetts Institute of Technology resides a unique robot who may be "growing a soul." The robot's name is "Cog." Cog is a remarkable attempt to create a machine that is not so machine-like. Cog amazes and frightens people because it behaves in an intriguingly human-like fashion. The people who work with Cog often face the temptation to refer to the robot as "he," though they have decided that the impersonal "it" is better, at least for now. Cog is different from almost all other attempts at artificial intelligence because it is developing, and doing so while in embodied interaction with the world around it. Cog was intentionally designed to mimic the learning processes of a real, embodied human being, and is beginning (and a meager beginning it is) to challenge those who argue that a machine can never achieve the unique behaviors of humans.[1]

Cog is different from most other attempts to model humans with machines for several reasons. The reasons relevant to our discussion are three: Cog is embodied, its processing is distributed, and its main programming consists of commands to seek input from its surroundings. Cog is an important project within the movement known as "Embodied Artificial Intelligence," which seeks to model more than simply human abstract computational problem-solving. Rather than consisting of just a "brain" that can play chess or manage inventory or mine data, Cog can hear, see, and touch. The robot was given an arm that mimics a human arm, two sensitive cameras for eyes and a microphone for ears. The creators designed it this way because they believe that human intelligence is the product of development in which a person experiences a physical environment, and they wanted to model the human development of intelligence.

Also to copy human knowing more faithfully, Cog was not designed with a central processing unit in which all data and commands are stored and processed. Rather, more like the human brain and nervous system, Cog has a number of different, autonomous processors that can communicate with one another. This allows the possibility for data in one processing unit to affect even the kind of data received in the others, as the robot arm might respond to visual stimuli by attempting to grab the ball offered by the engineer. With several processors affected both by the information received from the outside and from the other processors, the architecture is closer to that of the human nervous system, which is a massively interconnected network of nerves and nerve centers.

So that intelligence might develop, rather than simply be entered "whole" by some adult programmer, Cog's primary instructions are to seek data input from its environment (which is a lab room, so far). Something like this seems "programmed" into human infants, who are quintessentially curious, and very capable of absorbing and assimilating (in some sense) input from their surroundings. With this architecture and open-ended instructions, the engineers were very eager to switch Cog on and watch what happened. They have not been disappointed with the results because Cog's behavior has raised some very important questions and challenged many of the assumptions of the more traditional AI community.

Videotape of Cog shows the robot appearing to play with a ball, move a wooden block (knocking it to the floor, as a small child might), respond to different faces that enter the room, follow objects with its eyes, and imitate movements of human "playmates." These apparently "childlike" behaviors, however, should not necessarily be taken as evidence that the engineers have succeeded in reproducing any relevant feature of human learning. Cog's interconnected circuitry has already grown too complex for the engineers to know exactly what is going on in the production of many of these behaviors, so a good bit of the debate about the genesis of its responses is abstract and philosophical (and very enlightening). It is clear, however, that Cog's behavior is orders of magnitude less complex than even a very young human infant. But the project has provided a strong counterargument to those who insist that machines will never be able to duplicate important human behaviors. In a key sense, Cog exhibits behavior that is unmachinelike, in that it is learning, and it surprises its creators.

Cog has succeeded in gathering and assimilating information from its environment and utilizing that information in future encounters. Charles Peirce would probably say that it has developed a series of habits, or even primitive "beliefs," which are a type of habit. When one of its main programmers stands directly in front of Cog's eyes and nods, Cog nods in response (robot see, robot do?). It has acquired a habit. To the surprise of most analysts, however, Cog does not respond this way to every human face it sees (Cog seems confused by beards). It also will not nod when the human interactor covers part of his own face with a plate.[2] Cog has surprised its creators with many other more subtle behaviors, behaviors the team has no real hope of ever fully explaining in a straightforward mechanical-causal fashion. While we must be careful not to conclude too much about human-machine similarity, Cog does seem to be an example of mildly complex entity that has the ability to acquire new habits unpredictably and not totally explicably. Since this is a key feature of life and of humans, defenders of machine-human similarities have in Cog a useful intellectual weapon. At a very rudimentary level, Cog seems to be doing some baby-things, which have always been conceived differently than machine-things. Perhaps this is why most of Cog's attendants would feel moral qualms if they were ever required to unplug him.

A Painful Embarrassment?

In pointing out the degree to which humans have advanced beyond the apes, Nietzsche's *Zarathustra* reminds his listeners that to human beings, the ape is "a laughing-stock or a painful thing of shame."[3] Apes probably acquired this status not due to their distinctness from humans, but from an all-too-revealing similarity. The casual observation of chimpanzees at the zoo invariably leads one to affirm the manifold likenesses to humans. Both in appearance and in behavior, the chimps clearly make the closest approach to humans of any animal in the zoo. The more science learns about life and the genes that guide it, the more we see that these apparent superficial similarities are deeply grounded biologically. Deep resemblance is evident at whatever level one would care to explore, from large primate "nations" to the molecular biology of any individual "citizen." The most general reason why people have come to accept an evolutionary understanding of life on earth is the incredible similarities among living systems. Darwin and other founders of the theory were very impressed by it, and today molecular biology is finding comparable structural resemblance at microscopic levels. With chimps and humans, we can point to at least four levels of similarities that help to persuade scientists of our strong hereditary kinship.

Starting with the very smallest and most recently discovered level of resemblance, we now know that the DNA molecules of humans and chimpanzees are incredibly similar. Each variety of living thing has a signature DNA structure. The average human DNA molecule, for example, is made of up about 65 million pairs of bases (each itself a small molecule), arranged in such a way as to direct the formation of the proteins that will compose the various kinds of tissues that make a human body. The structure of the DNA molecule of chimpanzees is more than 98 percent identical to that of humans. These slight differences in the instructions for the synthesis of proteins make the difference biologically between humans and chimps. With this considerable hereditary likeness, it is not surprising that chimps look and behave a lot like us, both individually and corporately. We are made of the same stuff, the same kinds of molecules doing the same kinds of things.

It is not surprising that chimps have four limbs (with two able to be freed for grasping), binocular vision, organs and bones of the same shape and location as those of humans, very human-like neural circuitry, and other features. Neither is it surprising that the young chimps play rough games with each other, disturbing their mothers who are trying to clean them, while the father observes the scene from a nearby rock. Given this extreme DNA match, one might not be startled to learn that chimps even plan for the future and make tools, two behaviors long claimed to be the exclusive province of humans. It is not unheard of for a chimpanzee to strip leaves from a stick, thus making a tool for the extraction of termites, while still outside of visual contact with the mound where this tool will soon be used.[4] It is not surprising that the young chimps then learn from their parents the proper way to peel and eat fruit or to gather a stick full of juicy termites. The young ones imitate the mature ones, developing habits that will aid in their survival. And the behavioral habits extend well beyond the immediate "families," creating "cultural" practices that serve to distinguish one population of chimps from another. One group of chimps may not practice the "stick-termite" extraction method, while another group across the hill does. A wide range of behavioral differences between different groups of chimps has been documented by the collection of reams of data from a number of independently working researchers.[5]

These findings powerfully suggest that a rich cultural history exists within chimpanzee communities and that different communities have practices that are handed down from generation to generation. Many of the differences seem rather arbitrary, while others seem to be behavioral adaptations to specific environmental conditions. The parallel with human culture is obvious. There are thousands of little things that, for instance, Chinese people tend to do that Americans do not, and vice versa. In some countries slurping soup, belching, eating with your left hand, and resting your elbows on the table are social missteps, while these practices are perfectly acceptable in other countries. The nature and distribution of these alternate behaviors, at many different scales, seems very comparable to that being documented among the chimps (and other primate groups).

From DNA copying itself during cell division and gamete formation, to resemblance between father and child, to the passing on of family traditions, to formation and maintenance of cultural heritage, the world is taking on habits in every corner. Human beings provide no fundamental exception to this tendency. We are a lot like the apes, which are a lot like other mammals, which are like lower animals, which are like convection currents and water running down a rockface. The increasing complexity as one ascends the tree of life toward the human branch does make a difference (we can do a whole lot more than other primates), but the degree of continuity is striking. If you dissect an ape and a human down to the molecular level, you will find the same base pairs in molecules of DNA, making up the genes that direct the formation of all the other material within the organism. If you break down the tissue even further, you will find carbon, oxygen, hydrogen, nitrogen, and traces of other chemicals right from the periodic table. And you won't find anything else, either in the ape or the human.

Either/Or No More

Because we are learning more and more about the fundamental chemistry and physics of life, the twenty-first century will see headlines about advances in genetics more than about any other field in pure science. These advances will serve to confirm the crucial role played by heredity in shaping the material and the behavior of human beings. The human genome project is well on its way to mapping the 50,000 to 100,000 genes (segments of DNA molecules) that encode human structure. Everything from IQ to eye color, from shyness to stature will theoretically be detectable from the moment of conception or even sooner. Evidence will pile up that we are very much like a computer program, an embodied, interactive DNA-driven information process. Myriad human behaviors and characteristics once thought to require an immaterial soul will be shown to rely only upon astoundingly complex arrangements of very simple component parts. Memory, hope, convictions, love, poetry, and even spirituality will be shown to have strong connections to DNA and the biochemical processes it induces.

What will Christians make of announcements that persons lacking a certain gene arrangement have only a minuscule chance of ever having a religious experience? What will they make of further discoveries that locate ethical, artistic, and spiritual experiences in specific kinds of biochemical events? One option would be to ignore science and retreat into the bliss of not paying attention to the way that nature works, which would be unfortunate or even disastrous. Another option would be to challenge the conclusions of science when they appear to challenge cherished beliefs, which would be wonderful, as long as scientists and believers are willing to change their minds when the evidence becomes weighty enough. Even better would be a concerted effort by scientific and religious thinkers to expose the assumptions that inform the positions they hold, to examine the very foundations of the knowledge they claim to have. Any who do will invariably see that this world is never as simple as any of our simple statements describing it might seem to show. We will then further realize that utter humility is called for in drawing any sweeping conclusions about the broader meaning of this messy and complicated world. We will see that our binary thinking must be supplemented (or even supplanted) by careful but fuzzy thinking, that the "either/or" insisted upon by many famous dualisms must dissolve into beautifully complex portraits of a universe that forever moves through continuous shades of magnificent shapes and colors, tones and timbres, toward an end that we can now only vaguely imagine.

Mind, Soul, Self, and Body

Plato, in many ways the founder of the Western intellectual tradition, believed that the essence of humans was found in their souls, which were quite distinct from bodies. He viewed the body as the prison house of the soul and salvation as the soul's release from its incarceration in this unfortunately dirty and corruptible material form. René Descartes, in many ways the founder of the modern Western intellectual tradition, essentially agreed. He, too, argued that the essence of humans was not to be found in their material substance, but in their spiritual substance, which might be called mind, self, "I," or soul. For both Descartes and Plato, "mind stuff" was drastically different from "material stuff." Thus both of these thinkers were representatives of a school of thought known as "mind-body dualism." Christian theology in ancient and modern times has often adopted this very dualism, frequently viewing it as essential to the faith. The worldview of contemporary science is radically hostile to this dualism, and new discoveries continue to reinforce the belief that Platonic-Cartesian dualism is no longer tenable. Evolutionists' and geneticists' rejection of this dualism (and its cousin, the natural-supernatural split) is at the heart of many rifts between Christianity and science in the twentieth century. The "naturalistic" assumptions of these and other sciences are often thought to predispose their practitioners toward conclusions unfriendly to faith.

It must be noted that many very compelling, if not irrefutable, reasons have been given over the centuries for this dualistic understanding of human nature. The mind, obviously it seems, is not subject to the same kinds of effects and limitations as the body. The rich interior life of the human consciousness is not bound by the usual regularities of nature, from gravity to time to decay and death. Our minds can seemingly occupy different places and times, ideas and mental pictures can persist without degradation for decades. Imagination, mathematics, memory, value, logic, and a hundred other mind-functions bear very little resemblance to the material objects of our everyday existence. The part of me that can remember, learn, calculate, plan, love, and cherish seems very different from the parts of me that take nourishment, move me about from place to place, and deteriorate as I age. Furthermore, our sense of human value and the hope it engenders seem misguided if our hope must lie in these latter categories of human activity. The material parts of us will clearly go the way of all flesh. Every animal, including each of us, will die, and its matter will be returned to the natural rhythms of decay and recycling. If our souls matter more than all of this, then they must persist, so goes many a religious argument. There must be more to my future than to become food for the worms. Admittedly, this line of thought is more wishful thinking than argument, but it is powerful for many persons.

These lines of argument have been decimated in the nineteenth and twentieth centuries. In addition to the strong genetic claims of the kinship of all life previously discussed, brain science has made great progress in describing the physiological basis of those functions thought to require something more than neuronal firing. Brain injury and disease profoundly affect our remembering, our hoping, our loving, our planning, and our faith. The content of even my deepest convictions can be radically altered by a sufficient blow to my head. Like "The Man Who Mistook His Wife for a Hat,"[6] even our most committed relationships will suffer if disease ravages our higher brain function. Where is the core of selfhood in one so afflicted? If the soul, mind, or self is a nonmaterial entity, then how can a so obviously material cause alter the self so completely, and often so tragically?

Brain science, genetics, and related fields will continue to uncover the details of the connections between our "higher" selves and the material substrate on which they rely. Evolutionists will continue to uncover the details of our intimate relationship to the other animals and indeed to all life. A Platonic-Cartesian brand of mind-body dualism will become increasingly difficult to defend in the light of scientific progress. Does this mean, as Carl Sagan claims, that there is no use for talk of a "soul?" If such dualism is dead wrong, does this mean that anything essential is lost to the Christian faith? Absolutely not, because the anti-religious scientists who would make such claims are still presupposing the legitimacy of framing these questions on the presumptions of the dualism they deny. The dualisms of Plato and Descartes insist upon a radical discontinuity between body and soul, many materialistic opponents of these grant the discontinuity and then argue that there is no kind of "soul" stuff. But this is another example of an answer being inadequate because of the inadequacy of the question as formulated.

If we grant that everything that exists must be either mind stuff or matter stuff, then the contemporary scientific view of the world seems to be squeezing mind stuff out of the picture. But, as even Aristotle (Plato's star student) tried to show, this Platonic distinction is highly problematic in the first place. The Cartesian version of this dualism turns out to be even more problematic because it tries to reconcile the free will of the soul with the completely law-governed activity of the body, all the while presuming a modern, necessitarian view of natural law. Descartes believed that the body, which he admitted was made of matter, was subject to the same laws of nature as all the rest of the matter in the world. But the mind (self, soul, "I"), because it was not made of this law-governed stuff, was free. Then somehow it could initiate actions of the body, though he never succeeded in showing how this was even possible. Descartes knew that there were serious problems with his view, and it was challenged by other thinkers from day one. But he, like many of us, could not seem to get beyond the powerful impression that the laws of physics and chemistry do in fact govern our bodies, and the even more powerful impression that our minds can choose to direct the actions of those bodies. I can deliberate about eating a bagel, decide to eat it, then make my arms and hands deliver it to my mouth. I also could have decided on bacon and eggs, Choco-bomb cereal, or a banana. Did my DNA and years of environmental stimuli dictate the breakfast food decision? Do my DNA and environmental stimuli dictate the hundreds of more important decisions I must make? Or do I have a soul, an added nonmaterial component part that somehow "supernaturally" overrides natural regularities to endow me with a mysterious "free will?" Or is there a better way to think of "soul," a way that will not gore us with the horns of this ancient and modern dilemma? Genesis 2, with some interpretive help from Aristotle and Charles Peirce, provides just such a better way.

Mysterious Majestic Mudballs

Some of my Old Testament teachers would use the word "mudballs" to describe the understanding of human nature in Genesis 2. "The Lord God shaped the man out of the dust of the earth, breathed into his nostrils the breath of life, and the man became a living soul" (v. 7). The dust is *inspired*, literally "breathed into." This is no longer ordinary dirt; it is God-breathed dirt. Whenever it starts to breathe, it is because God breathed into it first. The dust was inspired and given the power to reproduce that inspiration generation after generation. Note that the verse does not say that God "placed" or "gave" or "added" a soul to the material thing just created. No, the Lord God breathed, and the man became a living soul. The soul is not something Adam *has*; it is rather something he *is*. He is an inspired mudball who owes it all to God the Creator. This is fundamentally not a dualistic reading of human nature and is therefore very consonant with many views of human nature offered by contemporary science. The dust of the earth is the collection of elements represented on the periodic table of the elements, or more fundamentally, energy or quarks, or whatever the latest consensus takes to be the fundamental stuff of the universe. Theologically, it does not matter what stuff is currently thought to be fundamental. Rather, it matters that this stuff is capable of being inspired by God to form amazingly complex and creative combinations, culminating on this planet in human beings, who alone among creatures are said to bear the image of the Creator.

Aristotle's view of the soul was much closer to this biblical view than was his teacher Plato's. For Aristotle, the soul was something like the "goal-directedness of the body."[7] Consistent with his overall understanding of reality and distinct from Plato's, Aristotle did not necessarily view a thing's essence as somehow separate from its actual embodiment. Any actual existing entity for Aristotle had to be a combination of matter and form, some kind of stuff in some kind of configuration. Updating his basic insight into the information age, we might suggest that the human being, like anything else, must be "informed matter." Each of us is made of some kind of material, but we are more than just the sum total of that material. We are more than the few dollars worth of laboratory chemicals that our separated elements might bring. Why are we more? A view consistent with Aristotle's and with the Genesis 2 creation narrative would say we are more, not because there is some separate added piece, a soul or essence, but due to the manner of organization of those basic elements. This manner of organization is not another added thing of the same order of thinghood as the parts that compose the whole, but is essentially information. Information, in this usage, is the way that matter is *in-formed*. It is the *form* that the matter is put *in*. This form, or manner of organization, changes as the person (or other complex entity) assimilates experiences, creating a developing story of a life. We may go further and, in opposition to the extreme reductionists, insist that this "information" is real, that it has the status of "thinghood" every bit as much as do the component parts. If we do so insist, we have taken a step toward affirming another philosophical position very dear to Charles Peirce, a "realism" that can be very friendly to the best of scientific and religious thinking.

A Cloud of Nominalists

The aeons-long debate between realists and nominalists appears at first glance to be exactly the abstract and irrelevant dispute that makes philosophers the victims of so many jokes. Yes, Plato wondered about whether something like "horseness" existed independently of actual individual horses. This debate is fundamentally about the nature of logic, and most discussions of it are highly technical and difficult, and there is little agreement about it today. Plato was a realist, believing that general names (such as horse, circle, red, etc.) referred to things that really existed. Aristotle thought they were real, but only insofar as realized in material things. Thus Aristotle's position moved more in the direction of nominalism, a position not usually thought to have been fully articulated until the fourteenth century in the work of English logician William of Ockham (1290–1349).

Ockham's position, nominalism proper, holds that the general, or category, or type names that we use in our symbolic communication are nothing but arbitrary names created by us to refer to perceived connections between individual members of some category. Thus whether we speak of horses, apples, truth, or justice, these type names do not refer to anything directly, hence nominalism, from the Latin root for "name." The only real things for the nominalist are the individual things. To generalize from individual things is not to find a new reality, it is merely to name an observed commonality, which is not as "real" as the actual things that have the commonality.

The groupings that might be so named vary widely. These names might be qualities (red, flat, hard, beautiful, etc.), category names (apple, horse, tree, planet, chair, etc.), natural laws (gravity, electromagnetism, relativity, conservation of momentum, etc., which name common features observed in events rather than things), or other collectives. The "realist" position in this debate holds that these general names do refer to something real. For example, the realist would hold that the law of gravity is something real, not simply a name devised to report on the common features of our experiences of falling things. It would be real even if no one ever named it.

Charles Peirce is something of a rarity in modern philosophy in that he is an avowed realist and sworn opponent of nominalism. According to

Peirce himself, almost every major philosophical mind since the Middle Ages was a nominalistic mind.[8] But for Peirce, the very scientific revolution that brought about the modern era should have caused a return to the older, realistic ways of thinking. This was because science's business was the uncovering of greater and greater generalities in nature. It found what it called "general laws," and asserted their reality. But a law is precisely the sort of thing denied reality by the nominalist position. Laws, patterns, or regularities had the character of a Platonic kind of "horseness," an abstract entity that later philosophers properly held in disdain, according to the nominalists. Perhaps the most extreme nominalists of the modern period were those Peircean opponents mentioned above, the logical positivists. They at least were consistent enough to admit the logical outcome of their nominalist convictions and did propose that laws, patterns, or regularities identified in nature were nothing more than systematic reports of observed events in nature.

For Peirce, such a position meant the end of knowledge, since it forbade the application of observed regularities to any situation that was not yet actual. For the nominalist, future events, because they have not yet happened, since they are not actual individual events that might be observed and named, cannot meaningfully be subsumed under any alleged pattern. For Peirce, if all we can do with our words and names is to report on the common features of events so far experienced, then that is not knowledge. Surely if you say that gravity attracts massive bodies toward each other, you do not mean only that you have made observations of a certain type, but that you expect future experiences of a certain type to have similar kinds of qualities. You are saying that patterns are real in the universe. You are claiming that the unobserved individual events will also conform to the patterns you saw in the observed events.

If Peirce is right, and these qualities and relations—granted only grudging and derivative status by nominalists—*are* real, then there is justifiable room to speak of "soul" without conflicting with even the most thoroughly scientific understandings of the human person. Peirce himself did not weigh in on this issue in this particular way, but it would be very consistent with his philosophy to think of the soul, mind, or self as the relationship of the myriad parts that make up a human being. This relationship of parts to each other, referred to earlier as their manner of organization, is just the sort of thing that might be granted reality by the realist and denied reality by the nominalist. As we have already seen, the parts that conspire to make a human are put together in a more complex manner than anything else we have yet discovered in the universe. The *information* of matter in this way can be thought of as real, even as a thing. Peirce also argues that these generalities, these conceptual "reals," can change. Nature's "laws," for example, have themselves evolved to reach their current state, in Peirce's view. So for Peirce, pattern, general, type, and regularity are real and dynamic. If this is right, then for the Christian, the "living soul" created from the dust of the earth may be understood as this kind of reality. It is not another thing, added like an extra organ, but the real and inspired relationship of specially capable parts to specially capable parts. For the committed nominalist, the parts have a claim to reality greater than that of the relationship between them. For the realist, this priority need not hold, and may even be reversed.

Atoms and Mudballs: God Bless the Dirt

The Great Smoky Mountains National Park is one of the earth's most beautiful places. My family and I often hike its winding trails, which is usually a muddy affair, since most of our favorite trails parallel stream beds. When we arrive home, we customarily leave our mud-caked hiking boots outside until the sticky and stubborn mud dries and can be pounded free. The children often must shed even more clothing, which has become soiled beyond recognition by an insatiable curiosity that must check beneath every wet rock that might conceal a salamander or other wonder.

If it has been a clear day, I ascend to my study to exercise the "philosopher's prerogative"—gazing out the window and at least giving the appearance of being lost in thought—and marvel at the majesty of the grandest of those mountains, which now rises in the distance to dominate the perceptions of the billions of living things that teem in its shadows. The words of the psalmist float through that window: "I will lift up my eyes to the hills. From where does my help come? My help comes from the Lord, maker of heaven and earth" (Ps 121:1-2). Then I fix my gaze downward, to a scene much closer but even further away, focusing on the haphazard pile of muddy shoes hastily abandoned at the doorstep a short time ago. The mud, still glistening with the mist that makes dust come to life, harbors mysteries as magnificent as the mountain itself. From that mud, from its carbon, nitrogen, hydrogen, oxygen, and assorted metals, a child can be woven. The atoms in that mud, the same kinds of atoms that comprise my children and you and me, have existed for billions of years. Some of them, in all likelihood, at one time were part of a person.

Jesus the Christ, in whom God was reconciling the world to God's self, was made of those same kinds of atoms, very old atoms. This muddy clay is no trivial, commonplace annoyance. This mud is spectacular, and we believe that God made it so. This mud is rich, pregnant with possibility. It is worthy of God's becoming, in Jesus, a mudball like us. This is the incarnation, God become mudball. To see ourselves as made of the same stuff that rests under our boots as we journey a mountain path is no insult to human dignity, no affront to the image of God in us; it is rather a reminder of the majesty of inspired mud, a reflected majesty that gives us but one more fleeting glimpse of the blinding brilliance of the maker of the mud.

In the Smoky Mountains life has grabbed a foothold in practically every square millimeter of space. The habits taken as the streams began carving their venous paths millions of years ago have allowed niches for the birth of a million more habits, creating a case study in biodiversity, the habit-taking virtuosity of a universe still taking cues from its Creator. The creek-veins of the mountains, the veins in the leaves of the trees and in the back of your hand, the trillions of pathways available to a single human nervous system, are each habits that were billions of years in the making. As habits themselves grope around for new habits, as they cooperatively combine to create even higher level and more interesting habits, faith has us expect that the best is yet to come. What new combinations, cooperations, or reconciliations can humans, the most complex instances of this creative habit-taking, anticipate? We cannot know exactly. Hopes for that kind of detailed certainty are gone. The world is too fuzzy for our predictions to tell us. But this fuzzy and uncertain world is likely the only kind that could have produced the panoply of forms that make our existence possible. This wondrous world of atoms and mudballs was possible only at the expense of great risk to a great number of individuals. The risk continues. If we are to live with faith in the potter who has created and urged the clay to where it is today, then we must engage in the creative risk, sharing in covenant with our Creator the self-emptying devotion that just might lead to a cross. We cannot know the specifics of what the future will hold, but, having the mind of Christ Jesus within us, we can have assurance that we have given our lives to the only thing that could ever really matter anyway.

> Therefore, if any one is in Christ, he is a new creation; the old has passed away, behold, the new has come. All this is from God, who through Christ reconciled us to himself and gave us the ministry of reconciliation; that is, in Christ God was reconciling the world to himself. (2 Cor 5:17-19a)

The new creation need not add anything to the mud. It could be a new way of inspiring the mud, causing its parts to work together more harmoniously and efficaciously in the reconciliation of the other mudballs to each other and to their inspirer. Mudballs then may work together, ever more inspired toward becoming part of new creation, a new heaven and earth, all made of the same or similar stuff that we wipe off of our shoes.

Notes

[1] For a good, brief discussion of Cog and some of its theological implications, see Anne Foerst, "Cog, a Humanoid Robot, and the Question of the Image of God," *Zygon. Journal of Religion and Science*, 33 no. 1 (March 1998): 91-111. Ms. Foerst is a theological advisor to the team developing the robot.

[2] For much more detailed information about the Cog project, visit Cog's web page at <www.ai.mit.edu/projects/cog>.

[3] Friedrich Nietzsche, *Also Sprach Zarathustra*, (Munich, Germany: Goldmann Verlag, 1990).

[4] Jane Goodall, *Through a Window. My Thirty Years with the Chimpanzees of Gombe* (Boston: Houghton Mifflin Company, 1990) 22.

[5] Reported in the British journal *Nature*, 17 June 1999.

[6] Oliver Sacks, *The Man Who Mistook His Wife for a Hat and Other Clinical Tales* (New York: HarperCollins, 1990).

[7] *De Anima*, Book II, ch. 4. He actually claims that the soul is the "entelechy" of the body. This is a very difficult concept, but something that has entelechy has its "goal within it." This whole book discusses various angles of this question.

[8] CP 1.19.

For Further Reading

Teilhard de Chardin, Pierre. *The Phenomenon of Man.* New York: Harper & Row, 1959.

Goodall, Jane. *Through a Window: My Thirty Years with the Chimpanzees of Gombe.* Boston: Houghton Mifflin Co., 1990.

Lakoff, George, and Mark Johnson. *Philosophy in the Flesh: The Embodied Mind and Its Challenge to Western Thought.* New York: Basic Books, 1999.

Sacks, Oliver. *The Man Who Mistook His Wife for a Hat and Other Clinical Tales.* New York: HarperCollins, 1990.

Chapter 9

Faith and Risk, Science and Kierkegaard

In the last two chapters I will try once again to reconcile apparently diverse arenas of human belief by discussing again the common features of Peircean scientific and passionate existentialist approaches to knowing and being. This time, however, the ideas will hover around those of the explicitly Christian father of existentialist thought and champion of faith, Søren Kierkegaard.

At first glance, the styles and conclusions of Peirce and Kierkegaard appear to contrast in the extreme. Kierkegaard was a passionate poetic spirit, an advocate of the subjective "leap of faith," and a sworn enemy of any who would elevate "objectivity" in knowledge to a privileged position. It would not be unfair, from the perspective of the nineteenth century, to join with those who labeled his work "anti-intellectual." Charles Peirce, on the other hand, was a tenacious proponent of the scientific method, a practicing scientist, and philosopher of math and logic, disciplines which existentialists often deride as antiseptic and cold. Peirce spent untold hours in the painstaking measurement of physical quantities, seeking the highest possible degree of mathematical precision. Thus did Peirce spend his days in meticulous pursuit of "truths" whose patent irrelevance, according to a Kierkegaardian reading, supposedly left the human heart numbed and lost.

We have already encountered an important idea shared by Peirce and the existentialists when, in chapter 4, we talked about the future orientation of all human knowledge claims. Peirce and the existentialists, from different perspectives, saw the knowledge we claim in the present as irreducibly shaped by our investment in the future. Moreover, for Peirce and a number of other philosophers, this future invoked to give shape to our present is incapable of being exhaustively and accurately known. It is fuzzy, always surprising us. This fuzziness of the future serves to point out common elements of these two intellectual traditions that are normally considered to be at odds with one another. So maybe the worlds of the existentialist and the scientist are not really hopelessly opposed after all. By looking a bit more closely at a few key notions of Kierkegaard, the existentialist man of faith, and Peirce, the mathematical man of science, we can see further how the end of certainty suggested by recent work in the sciences provides an opportunity to develop a coherent and unified vision of the human quest for a transforming truth. We can see some more specific ways in which the end of certainty invites the person of faith to the adventure of covenant.

Kierkegaard and the Sterility of Objectivity

"We need money, so let's pray to God that He will help us," said a father to his young daughter, in an effort to teach her the efficacy of prayer and the faithfulness of God to God's children. So every morning the mother and father led the little girl in a prayer that God that would improve their financial situation. Then every afternoon they would check the mailbox for "manna," to see if there was a heaven-sent, U. S. Postal Service-delivered, gift. Sure enough, praise God, one day there was a check in the mailbox for several hundred dollars. The family thanked God for answered prayer. The little girl had asked God for help, and the rock of her salvation had come through. They told her that "the fervent prayer of a righteous man availeth much" (Jas 5:16 KJV).

This is a true story, but not the whole story. In this case the parents knew all along that the check was forthcoming. They knew that their tax refund was on the way, but were uncertain about the timing of its arrival. Of course, the innocent child was unaware of IRS procedure and was led to believe that her devout supplication had made the difference. In a remarkable instance of theological child abuse (not punishable by law, thankfully, due to U.S. separation of church and state), they had persuaded her to expend her fledgling spiritual energies in service of a foregone conclusion. I wonder still if she ever discovered her parents' subterfuge.

This may seem like an extreme example, but it discloses an important implication of many a worldview that fails to recognize the end of certainty. If the little girl had discovered this parental priming of the pump, she might well have developed a very justifiable resentment of their deceptive claim that her actions actually changed the course of events. In the parents' minds, at least, the story was already written, and nothing the daughter would do could change the outcome. If she had learned more of the truth of this episode, then the real lesson would have been about the futility of prayer. Similarly, if the story of the universe is already written, whether by divine intention or by nature's obedience to mathematically necessary mechanical laws, then the future is, in an important sense, already "recorded." It has no qualitative distinctness from the past, and our alleged choices are eternally scripted episodes in what would be best described as a Stoic tragicomedy. It will never be possible, with human thought configured as it is now, to conclusively refute either the scientific or theological necessitarianism that underlies most human dreams of certainty, but the price paid for such a view is very high and, as we have seen in chapter 3, the evidence in its favor is far from convincing.

Søren Kierkegaard (1813–1855) wrote passionately in rebuttal to a philosophical opinion that saw the world as the necessary unfolding of divine logic. He was very impressed at the deductive virtuosity of the creators of these magnificent philosophical systems, but he criticized them for ignoring the very concrete situation of the existing, developing, human being. He saw these sophisticated descriptions of a logically necessary universe as illegitimate attempts to escape the inherent uncertainty of the world actually inhabited by persons. For him, the attempt to describe a world that could be known with objective certainty was not a movement of faith. So he became history's most ardent apologist for subjectivity as truth.[1]

In many ways Kierkegaard was reacting to the scientifically inspired necessitarianism of the early modern period (though there were many other recipients of his attacks). He did not consider the desired goal of scientific inquiry to be sufficient for the life of faith, if that goal was to reach objective certainty. For Kierkegaard, faith required committing our lives to an objective uncertainty. Only thus does our attitude deserve the name "faith." Among his most famous dictums is, "Without risk, there is no faith."[2] If the universe is as the speculative philosophers would have it, a logically necessary unfolding of eternally scripted events, and if humans were capable of uncovering portions of the script, then the enterprise of uncovering these truths is an attempted escape from the life of faith. If the universe (and the mind of God, for that matter) resembles some grand equation, no less necessary for its apparent subtlety, then it inspires no covenantal commitment. It would require only as much devotion as, say, the Pythagorean theorem. Geometrical theorems do not inspire the kind of self-sacrificial devotion that is the heart of the Christian faith.

Now Kierkegaard does not challenge the validity of "objective" truth in itself. There may be a place in the grand scheme of things for mathematical certainty, but not, for Kierkegaard, in any discussion of issues of deep importance to existing human beings. Our life-shaping commitments are not to the objective validity of a theorem or argument, but to those things that are famously uncertain, such as marriage, children, and ultimately, religion. Our deepest commitments in these areas are the ones that excite our passions, that engage our embodied, existing, concrete selves. For Kierkegaard's faith-driven understanding of the world and of our knowledge of it, the objectivity (or certainty) of a mathematical proposition "is given, but for that reason the truth of such a proposition is also an indifferent truth."[3] Once truths like those of mathematics and related disciplines become settled to the satisfaction of the inquirer, reason demands an audience with the next paradox, the next unknown that lurks beyond the boundaries of objectivity. God, the ultimate being and mystery, is also ultimate paradox, a kind of paradox of paradoxes, the final goal of humans who try to think the thought that cannot be thought.[4] So faith is the commitment of one's self to something that is unavoidably an objective uncertainty.

In Kierkegaard's day, this line of thinking was in direct opposition to the scientific spirit that sought to "objectify" all knowledge in service of the persistent optimism of the certainty-seekers. He seemed to be saying that even if you grant the rational-scientific spirit the conclusions it was competent to draw, that the issues of faith and ultimate commitment remained untouched. Our supreme and broadest commitments were always going to reach beyond the realm of the objective, the certain. So he called upon Christians to make a "leap of faith" by committing themselves to the objectively uncertain, which was like jumping backwards into complete darkness, not knowing whether the leap would result in salvation or annihilation.[5] Since making such a commitment was beyond the province of reason, it must be a leap into the complete unknown. Once the leap has been made, new vistas are opened and the fear and trembling presumably transforms for the leaper into a transrational assurance of faith, but this assurance emphatically cannot be seen prior to leaping. Prior to leaping, all we see is darkness, a radical uncertainty that is the antithesis of scientific objectivity. Not only are the eyes of faith prevented from looking into a crystal ball, but they are also forbidden from peering into a fuzzy ball. Real faith is not the comfortable assent to propositions that are foregone conclusions; it is the passionate hurling of one's self into a future about which one can only guess. Thus the life of faith is irretrievably risky.

Kierkegaard Today?

Many of Kierkegaard's frontal assaults on objective, scientific kinds of knowing would flounder today for lack of a target, because the world as seen by the kinds of scientific eyes described in the previous chapters is much more friendly to his insistence on uncertainty and faith. Many scientists and most philosophers today harbor no real hopes of a human approach to the kind of objective certainty so thoroughly vilified by Kierkegaard. Uncertainty, some of it caused by the unavoidably subjective interference of the knower, has crept into even hard scientific disciplines. Even a number of purely mathematical processes fail to yield predictable outcomes.[6] Kierkegaard, presumably, would have to alter his attack today, in light of the new and uncertain sciences of the twentieth century. Some kind of faith, understood as a commitment of one's self to a future that is to some degree unknown and unknowable, is required of any who would make knowledge claims, including scientific claims. So the sciences as portrayed in our study are no longer endemically antagonistic to faith as understood by Kierkegaard. More than ever before, they reinforce the notion of a fuzzy future that makes some sort of faith a necessary part of any human project.

The lure of certainty, of a kind of objectivity modeled on the sciences of the modern period, persists. There are still many who seek to achieve pure and certain objectivity. We see many persons still clinging to the notion that their words, concepts, and numbers are directly and accurately representative of a reality beyond their own minds. In the evolution-creation debate, for example, extremists from both sides were portrayed as very sure of themselves and of the literal reference of their language. There are scientists who are trying to demonstrate that the universe spontaneously sparked into existence out of nothing, and Christians trying to prove their faith to an unbelieving world by showcasing a lab-coated "scientist" wielding a plank claimed to be from Noah's ark. In these cases and more, Kierkegaard's warnings about the antagonism of proof and faith are every bit as valuable today as they were in the first half of the nineteenth century.

Even though contemporary science and philosophy are reaching a consensus that nothing about the concrete world in which we live can strictly be proven, there are nevertheless a large number of systems that are so regular, so predictable, that we practically assume that their behaviors are proven. The sun will rise tomorrow, I will burn my hand if I extend it into a fire, and I will pay taxes and eventually die. The check from the IRS will come in the mail. For good or for ill of human beings, gravity will still operate tomorrow, propelling one skier to thrilling velocities and claiming the life of another. These near certainties, practically assured to continue, are not the objects of self-sacrificial faith. We do not put our lives on the line in trusting gravity or Newton's "laws" of motion. The foregone conclusions we presume to attend these long-established regularities do not call for courageous commitment. The position of Pluto in the year 2017 is predictable to any imaginable useful degree of precision. And this predictability makes the affirmation of its position "an indifferent truth."

Contrast that prediction with one that says "til death do us part." A marriage vow means so much more to us than a prediction about the physical location of a dead rock because the vow involves very unpredictable creatures and because the ones predicting their own fidelity have the ability to affect the accuracy of the prediction. I expect that in 2017 my wife and I will still love each other, that a grandchild or two will help fill our lives, and that our sons will be creative and fulfilled members of the human spiritual community. These predictions are quite vague and fuzzy, and many things could happen that could make them just plain wrong. But Pluto, the dead rock, will be just where the star atlas says it will be. Reverting to a very revealing Peircean phraseology, the reason for the differences between predictions involving humans and those involving Pluto is the fact that Pluto is not on the cutting edge of habit-taking, whereas the unbelievably complex human organism is. Humans can magnify microscopic influences into visible events; rocks generally cannot. Humans are far-from-equilibrium; rocks are not. Intense relationships between humans are farther from equilibrium and even more unpredictable. Our habits are not settled yet; Pluto's habits are fixed. It has carved out its channel in the stream bed of solar-system space. Committing ourselves only to near certainties, or pseudocertainties, is like placing a wager on the position of Pluto in 2017. No one will take the bet.

Let us not forget, however, that we cannot be completely sure that Pluto's orbit will remain consistent. A large comet could hit it, or hitherto undiscovered effects of the sun might cause calamitous results for the distant rock. Also remember that the predictions about its precise location cannot be made arbitrarily precise. We can predict its location for all intents and purposes that we can imagine, but we cannot locate it down to the millimeter. There are too many different effects to consider for us to pin it down exactly. With complex systems such as those discussed in chapters 6-8, the unpredictability is magnified to the degree that causes us to affirm the end of certainty.

Ein, Zwei, Drei, Kokolorum or "Abracadabra"

It may seem a strange pathology, and not a little paradoxical, to write a whole book about how little we know for sure about the universe, about the deep inadequacies of even our most widely accepted means of gaining knowledge. Yet I wish to argue that it is a perfectly appropriate stance of faith and reason to maintain that we humans really do not know very much at all about the universe. It seems that every new discovery raises more questions than it answers and teaches us a new lesson in just how limited our sight really is. These most tested and trusted means of finding something really true or beautiful have served rather to expose our ignorance. In Socrates' or Kierkegaard's minds, this situation should be no surprise. Socrates' only self-confessed wisdom was that he had an acute awareness of just how little he knew. For Kierkegaard, human reasoning powers will always "seek a collision."[7] It will seek the next unknown with an insatiable hunger for a mystery beyond a mystery, so it is to be expected that the cutting edge of learning would be inspired by the unexplained and drawn to the inexplicable.

We do not have to look very far to find a mystery that can paralyze our puny minds. Our universe is not only stranger than we normally think, but it is also stranger than we are able to think. The God whom we praise as its creator is likewise mysterious beyond our comprehension and imagination. In faith we believe that God has revealed God's self in the person of Jesus. Jesus is our best clue to the nature of God, and no existing person has Jesus completely figured out. We take a stab in the dark, a leap of faith, a guess at the riddle, which, if it approaches the truth, helps us to bring it all together and gives us a story and a picture of the universe by which we can orient our engagement with the future. It can give us new habits that may serve very well amid the unknown trials that will come to pass. This guess, leap, or stab in the dark is the most modestly supported of claims. We cannot prove it because it is invariably shot through with the fuzzy future. Our broadest faith claims are guesses so far exceeding the reach of anything called "data" that it may seem laughable that we even dare speak of God or of truth at all. We are incredibly far from grasping and comprehending the final word, but faith gives assurance that we are moving toward that final word.

Yet every age has seen those who would claim to have a special audience with the Speaker of the Final Word and a special hotline that overrides the standard interpretive filters of average human beings, removing all of the "static" that comes with linguistic expression and embodied, developmental thinking. Our humble assessment of human knowing inspired by the philosophical and scientific developments of the contemporary era suggest that those who claim to have this special access to the final word on some important human issue are really only fooling themselves (and maybe a few who listen to them). Whether this final word be conceived as a mathematical description of some crucial physical property, as an utterance of God somehow delivered to virgin human ears, or as arriving through some other vehicle of finality, the content of that "final" word exists as an evolving sign in the consciousness of a changing, growing, dying, and sinful human being. This human being can pretend to transcend his unfinished finitude, coming to dwell in the unsullied purity of abstract truth. He can say "abracadabra" or *ein, zwei, drei, kokolorum*[8] and imagine himself transformed into the abstract and immutable. He might also pretend to be magically transported to the moon's most majestic mountaintop. Such pretending does not disembody the pretender or confer upon him unfiltered access to realms above. Even if God said "IT," by the time "IT" makes its way into a human's biochemically constructed conscious self, that person has no guarantee that it bears any relevant resemblance to the divinely uttered "original." His/her affirmation of a conceptual "IT," which resides and changes amid the clutter and beauty of an historically conditioned self, finally "settles" nothing. If "IT" has any content at all for the human person, it is a belief-habit, ready for application and adjustment as it forges ahead toward the fuzzy future.

I can pretend to occupy the heavenly throne and share with the Creator some sort of God's-eye-view of the universe, even bellowing in despotic tones a report on this "absolute" truth that I behold, but in doing so I take a large bite out of the fruit that was forbidden in the ancient garden, the fruit whose arrogant consumption brought pain and death to the human spirit. Only God can have a God's-eye-view, and if I presume to share this perfected vision, then I arrogantly and tragically make a god of myself. Clearly this is a position for which I am desperately unqualified because, as I am reminded daily, sometimes I am wrong. My beliefs today are, I trust, closer to the final word than they were yesterday. I also trust that they will be even closer tomorrow, the next day, and so on. For Peirce and for Kierkegaard, we put ourselves and others in grave danger by insisting that our knowledge claims must never change (which is to insist that the future can theoretically be witnessed through a crystal ball), because the developing world presents to our visage only a cloudy future, whose fuzzy images gain clarity only through time, and partly through our choices in giving them shape. The God of our covenant has entrusted us to share the task of resolving these fuzzy images, creating along with God the masterpiece that will be the Kingdom of God. Many brushstrokes are yet to be realized, and we must not forget that masterpieces come in many, many different styles.

So are we left in a state of abject and hopeless ignorance? Can there be no vision of truth, no word of God for us today? Of course there can be.

To see how, we can seek counsel again from the poet and from the logician. We can take the best of what we can know about those fuzzy images (science) and set a course for those encounters that will help us bestow upon that future a shape more like one willed by God. We can take that leap of faith that orients us toward the fuzzy future with courage and conviction. We can take a guess at the riddle and let the guess guide us toward that final word, the ultimate *logos*. We can *believe*, in a sense affirmed by both Kierkegaard and Peirce and welcomed by an atmosphere of uncertainty that science has breathed into the intellectual community in the twentieth century. But what shall we believe? An often repeated criticism of Kierkegaard's approach to faith is that it can give no guidance about which leap to take.

Faith and Relativism

If a leap of faith is completely blind, if there is nothing but darkness in the region where we would leap, then how can we tell which leap to take? Kierkegaard does not address this question in just this way, but it raises a valid concern about his notion of the leap. If there is no "reason" why the Christian should take the leap to trust the incarnate Christ, then there would be no "reason" why the erstwhile leaper should not leap into belief in some other religious tradition, or a new cult, or some bizarre personal belief system. His exaggerated emphasis on individual subjectivity leaves him open to this criticism because if my faith decisions are mine and mine alone, rooted in an inwardness inaccessible to any other being, then it seems that anything goes. If I hold an objective uncertainty with the infinite passion of inwardness, then this is truth for Kierkegaard. I could affirm with the infinite passion of inwardness any manner of absurdity. I might confess "Frisbee-ism," the belief that after death my soul lands on the roof and will not come down. Are there any constraints at all on what I might believe? Does truth not have any objective component at all?

If we could get Peirce and Kierkegaard together, they might be able to work out a theory of belief that could answer this criticism. They could agree that the world is uncertain and that the things that matter the most to us are precisely the things that are the most uncertain. They could agree that humans and their beliefs are concretely existing things and that humans and their beliefs are in a constant state of change, development, and it is hoped, growth. They could agree that this developmental aspect of human existence makes the human an unsettled and unfinished work. The future is uncertain and requires faith if it is to be engaged courageously. They could agree that God and the universe conceal mysteries too deep for us even to begin to comprehend. They would disagree, however, on the assessment of what Kierkegaard called "objective" knowledge.

Even Peirce's meticulous gathering of gravimetric data, for Peirce, mattered a great deal. The predictions of planetary movement and falling rocks on earth were not for Peirce "an indifferent truth." On Peirce's understanding of belief, even these kinds of quantified results had some potential bearing on future practical action, and since this future action might prove the belief unwarranted, holding the belief requires a sort of faith in a future whose precise contours are unknown and inaccessible to us. Scientific thinking, for Peirce, was future-oriented just like other kinds of thinking, and it was vitally important to the future well-being of persons. The detailed analysis of nature from a thousand different angles had the potential to provide information that would have practical application in some potential future. If "discoveries" proved unhelpful, then they would be adjusted to accommodate the new experiences.

So Peirce would not concur with Kierkegaard's mutual exclusion of subjective and objective. All belief is both. A belief is a person's habit that will guide the person's interaction with the future world. There must be a person and a world in order for there to be a belief. For Peirce, the world of nature was stubborn. Honest and conscientious inquirers repeatedly are forced to adjust their beliefs (habits) in the face of the world's challenges to existing beliefs. The universe continually keeps us from affirming that "anything goes." There are regularities in nature, according to Peirce, but they are not eternally changeless and mechanical laws. These regularities continue to impress themselves upon the minds of those who have a true desire to understand them. If we fancifully try to create our own beliefs about the world out of nothing, then the world will confront us with experiences that contradict our concocted theory. If we are not primarily concerned with discovering the truth, but with advancing our pet theory, then our minds can strenuously try to adapt apparently conflicting experiences to the theory in question. There have always been people who prefer their own belief systems to nature's stubborn insistence that we adapt to its patterns, but these are precisely the people who are labeled as prejudiced, biased, or nonobjective.

At this point we should sense a disconnect with Kierkegaardian terminology. "Objectivity," for Kierkegaard, is a perspective that does not involve the concrete, existing individual and is therefore foreign to the life of faith. But for Peirce and other contemporary advocates of scientific modes of thought, there is a strong resemblance between "objectivity" and "selfless devotion." If our concern is really to move toward the truth, then we will get out of the way and let the truth shine through. We will not allow our own wishes about how things ought to be to become obstacles to understanding the way things are. Our beliefs, or thought-habits, will be shaped by our contact with the world in its entirety, and if our desire is the truth, we are willing to change those thought-habits when our honest assessment of experience compels us to do so. For Peirce, this honest and courageous engagement of the future must take place within community, if the march toward truth would proceed.

To move toward the final word, to learn about our universe, requires the coordinated quest of a committed community. Each member of this committed community is concerned with discovery; not self-aggrandizement, prestige, power, wealth, or position. Each will intensely turn himself or herself into a magnifier of the truth, encouraging others likewise to lose themselves, to become transparent to the ultimate *logos*. The scientific insistence on objectivity, understood in this way, is a demand for faithfulness itself. Objectivity has been reinterpreted as intersubjectivity, where the world and the rest of the questing community constrain us from taking just any leap we want, at least if we honestly want to know and serve the truth. This kind of objectivity, because it requires a risky openness to possible future refutation, the commitment of one's energies to discovery of truths beyond one's personal desires, and the honest and intense commitment to the community of inquirers, looks a lot like faith. It is not by accident that I describe Peirce's idealized scientific community with language that could easily apply to an idealized church. The two kinds of communities have much in common, similarities that can be seen more clearly if we examine more closely Peirce's notions of belief and truth.

Notes

[1]*Concluding Unscientific Postscript,* trans. David F. Swenson and Walter Lowrie (Princeton NJ: Princeton University Press, 1941) 169ff.

[2]Ibid., 182.

[3]Ibid.

[4]*Philosophical Fragments,* trans. David Swenson (Princeton NJ: Princeton University Press, 1936) 46.

[5]*Concluding Unscientific Postscript,* 90ff. Kierkegaard's penetrating psychological analysis of this leap will not be treated here, but the reader will be richly rewarded for grappling with these sections of the *Postscript.*

[6]See the work of, for instance, Gregory Chaitin, pioneer in the search for randomness in mathematics. An accessible introduction to some of his ideas can be found in "Randomness in Arithmetic," *Scientific American,* 259 (July 1988): 80-85.

[7]*Philosophical Fragments,* 46.

[8]*Concluding Unscientific Postscript,* 169, 177.

Chapter 10

Hoped For
and Unseen

There are many other aspects of Peirce's philosophy that might profitably be examined for their possible benefit to the life of faith. Our study will conclude with a brief look at a few of these. Peirce's ideas of truth, fallibilism, belief/habit, and "the guess" have all been referred to in the preceding pages, along with other key elements of his thought. However, there are still more directions in which these fruitful notions might be developed as ways to understand a faith that seeks a roadway over, around, and through the challenges and opportunities that this uncertain world will almost surely deliver.

Truth and Reality

Charles Peirce spoke of the true and the real as follows: "The opinion which is fated to be ultimately agreed to by all who investigate, is what we mean by the truth, and the object represented in this opinion is the real."[1] This understanding of truth is consistent with Peirce's overall theory of meaning in which the meaning of any concept is the expectation of its future application to a practical situation. The truth about any matter is the beliefs that would be held by the committed inquirers when all of the trials are done, when all of the experiments have been run. For Peirce, the object of this sign, that to which it refers, is the real. Truth never escapes sign-existence; it resides, even in the end, as signs in the minds of the community of inquirers. The object of these true signs are what he means by "reality." Truth is no less true for its being located in the indefinitely distant future. Reality is no less real just because we cannot inhabit the future whose truth will describe it.

Peirce's is an intriguing and controversial understanding of truth and is another example of a principle that can never be summarily demonstrated as correct. But it may provide a workable and substantial middle way between the relativism of complete subjectivity and the dogmatism of those who have bewitched themselves into believing they have achieved a God's-eye-view. Like all definitions and beliefs, the way to determine the strength of this view of truth is to "try it on." Socrates was among the first to try on a version of Peirce's notion of truth, albeit in a very rudimentary fashion. If we could engage Socrates in this discussion, I think he would agree with Peirce's further reflections on his future-located understanding of truth. Peirce says,

> There is nothing, then, to prevent our knowing outward things as they really are, and it is most likely that we do thus know them in numberless cases, although we can never be absolutely certain of doing so in any special case.[2]

For Peirce and Socrates, truth has a real object, but we cannot be certain in any specific case that the notion we entertain at the moment is actually the one corresponding to that object, the real. Likewise, Socrates did not claim to know any final truths, but he made a courageous guess that organized his experience for him and gave him a direction to move and had faith that he was in fact moving toward that truth that so far eluded his grasp.

It seems as though science has increasingly improved its understanding of the universe, as the weight of evidence offered by stubborn experience has pushed persons toward common opinions where once there was contention and disagreement. The flat-earthers and geocentrists are gone. Everyone agrees that genes are DNA sequences that encode proteins in myriad ways to produce living organisms and that the structure of any individual's DNA is mostly dictated by the structure of the parents' DNA. Earlier speculations about the functions of heredity have been abandoned in the face of this scientific advance. Aristotle, for example, thought that sperm cells were small versions of the organism that they would beget, and that, presumably, a bull's sperm cell that was missing a leg would yield an equivalently deformed offspring. We have come a long way since then, even if science has been heavily influenced by social factors (such as a model of rationality that is predisposed to favor the interests of white, male Europeans). Scientific rationality clearly has been influenced by arbitrary social factors, but nature's patterns have a stubborn persistence that eventually debunks ideological bias in "scientific" theories, and attention paid to these patterns by persons honestly seeking to see how the world works has given us better theories today than we had yesterday.[3]

A generous reading of the history of religious communities might lead to a similar interpretation of their progress, though any conclusions here are even harder to defend than in the scientific disciplines. Still, people used to justify slavery, genocide, racism, sexism, and nationalism on religious grounds to a greater extent than they do today. We no longer think of God as a very powerful human being with a deep voice and very large brain. Most denominations within Christendom no longer reserve salvation only for themselves. Of course, there are plenty of exceptions to these generalizations. However, we could argue that even if these instances of progress are the exception, they might be the exceptions in which the community of the committed has really taken seriously the call to get out of the way of the truth, to engage in an unbiased quest to discover the truths of God. The counterexamples, including religious hatred that may even lead to genocide, could be cited as examples of persons pursuing an agenda other than the truth that is fated to be agreed upon by the community of conscientious seekers. Religious bigots, for example, are making themselves willfully blind to the mountain of commonalities they share with their hated enemies. If religious (or any other) communities really worked together, testing and reproving each others' beliefs in an attempt to improve their communion with the ultimate truth, really were open to adjusting those beliefs in light of challenges wrought by future practical experience, then these communities could take positive strides toward discovering and revealing the truth that awaits believers at the end. They would also realize that they could be wrong about any number of beliefs that separate them from their neighbors, which in turn would make them much more likely to see their would-be opponents as fellow travelers trying to find their own best way to the truth. They would thereby be much less likely to behave hatefully or murderously toward their counterparts.

The Fallibility of Infallibility

The "Peircean" approach to learning and growing is profoundly humble. It is "fallibilistic" in that it insists that all seekers be open to new experiences that may bring about reevaluation of important beliefs. A fallibilist, like Socrates, is not certain enough of his conception of truth or goodness or beauty to bring harm to another. In Plato's early dialogue, *Euthyphro*, Socrates chides a young zealot for his excessive certitude in a matter of life and death. The youthful Euthyphro has filed murder charges against his own father in the case of a death of a slave, a case in which it is not at all clear that the father intended for the slave to die. But Euthyphro is so convinced of his own understanding of goodness that he is willing to have his father convicted. Throughout the course of the dialogue Socrates tears down the exaggerated confidence of the young man, while sarcastically claiming a desire to learn goodness from someone who, unlike Socrates himself, is so sure of the godly course of action.

Socrates' own commitment to goodness and truth is no less intense than Euthyphro's, but Socrates' love of the good compels him to be humble in any attempt to express it. Socrates committed his life to the belief that there really is goodness, all the while never claiming to have a fixed and clear understanding of it. This humility of Socrates leads to the most important distinction between himself and Euthyphro: Socrates was willing to sacrifice himself in service to his deepest convictions, but he was not willing to sacrifice someone else. The courage of his convictions and the vindication of his philosophy took center stage in a world-changing drama as he drank the poison and died, executed by the state whose leaders valued their own political status above a humble and honest search for the truth, a search whose honesty threatened to reveal their hypocrisy to the world. Socrates valued his service to "the god" more than his own life, and important strands of Western history have vindicated his guess. It is no wonder that Western literature is replete with comparisons of Socrates and Jesus.

Peirce the scientist was vehemently opposed to any practice that "blocked the road to inquiry." Exaggerated certitude did just that. The conviction that one has it all figured out, or has spoken and understood the final word regarding any matter, shuts off further learning and growth in that area. First, it stifles dialogue. One who is so sure he or she understands precisely God's words or is persuaded beyond the shadow of a doubt that one theory captures "the way things are," has no need of further discourse with detractors. Hence community is broken, perhaps the very community that is itself a prerequisite for the improvement of our beliefs, the approach to that final consensus by which Peirce defines truth. Plato does not tell us if Socrates succeeded in puncturing Euthyphro's bubble of certitude. Socrates, though, was acting in the spirit of fallibilism and of Peircean truth in making strenuous efforts to continue the dialogue that would keep the "road to inquiry" open.

Habit, Faith, and Belief

One of the defining debates in Christian theology in the twentieth century has been between those who define Christian "belief" primarily as assent to a body of propositions and those who, like Kierkegaard, see it primarily as a subjective relationship of commitment. Each side accuses the other of abandoning central elements of the faith. The propositionalists accuse the "relationship" side of a muddy existentialist relativism where anything goes, as long as one is committed to something. Kierkegaardians accuse the propositionalists of a wooden and arrogant dogmatism. Both of these characterizations contain at least a germ of truth, as evidenced by countless souls lured by the divergent temptations either to water down the faith or to turn it to stone. Clearly relativism that can claim nothing and dogmatism that pretends to have a God's-eye-view of truth should be avoided. Peirce's understanding of belief provides a way to avoid both of these pitfalls while at the same time illuminating the often obscured common ground shared by these two positions.

As we have seen, belief for Peirce is a habit of mind that creates for its holder a strategy for dealing with future practical situations. Beliefs become fixed when the practical situations they confront provide no reason to change them. Our belief that gravity attracts is quite fixed, since we all live daily with gravity, and gravity is one of nature's processes that has become (all but) fully habituated. Large collections of atoms in relatively simple combinations and relationships, like those in rocks, do not often exhibit surprising behavior, and we have become accustomed to expecting rocks and planets to behave very predictably. So our practical experience every day does not provide us with a reason to change that belief. There is no obstacle that keeps that particular belief-habit from digging its channel ever deeper into our psyches. Other beliefs are quite changeable. For instance, I believe that my child will play a little league baseball game tonight. I will continue to believe this until such a time as some event, such as a thunderstorm, causes me to alter that belief.

By now, Peirce's famous statement of his view of belief should be easily comprehended.

> And what, then, is belief? It is the demi-cadence which closes a musical phrase in the symphony of our intellectual life. We have seen that it has just three properties: First, it is something that we are aware of; second, it appeases the irritation of doubt; and, third, it involves the establishment in our nature of a rule of action, or, say for short, a habit. As it appeases the irritation of doubt, which is the motive for thinking, thought relaxes, and comes to rest for a moment when belief is reached. But, since belief is a rule for action, the application of which involves further doubt and further thought, at the same time that it is a stopping-place, it is also a new starting-place for thought. That is why I have permitted myself to call it thought at rest, although thought is essentially an action. The final upshot of thinking is the exercise of volition, and of this thought no longer forms a part; but belief is only a stadium of mental action, an effect upon our nature due to thought, which will influence future thinking.[4]

In this understanding of the nature of belief we can see the common ground occupied by the existentialists and the propositionalists. For Peirce, every proposition that someone believes is already a plan for a concrete action. Our beliefs are exactly our plans to act or react in a specified fashion when the appropriate situation arises. We feel the irritation of doubt when we are unsure how we would approach a potential situation. In doubting, our thought processes search out a rule for action that appeases the irritation, and we rest in that rule of action, or habit, until some event triggers a new episode of doubt. If it rains tonight, then I will have to come up with a new belief to replace the one that expected to attend a baseball game. If when I arise from bed tomorrow my body levitates and attaches to the ceiling, then I might have to reconsider that habit of expecting to be pulled earthward, though in this latter case I would check out other possibilities first because the gravity-belief is not one to be abandoned readily.

So every belief is connected to concrete existence in some way, if it has content at all. Even the so-called "objective" truths so mistrusted by Kierkegaard, on Peirce's view, are not removed from the action-plans or projects of individual, embodied human beings. If they are so removed, if they are nothing but verbal affirmations with no potential practical bearings, then they are not beliefs at all; they are empty utterances. But these beliefs are also grounded in the believer's concourse with a stubborn world. This universe simply will not permit the honest belief that the expectation of gravity is unfounded. Our habits, like the habits of stream beds and convection currents, take root and grow in a physical universe that has real properties. This world will not justify a devoted truth-seeker's affirmation of frisbeeism or flat-earthism or any number of other fantastical beliefs. We cannot be certain that we possess the truth regarding these real properties of things, but the consistency and stubbornness of the world strongly suggest that reality and the truth that would signify it in the minds of humans are *not* mere arbitrary constructions that could have taken any shape.

Serious scientific and religious thinkers have reason to applaud this notion of belief. It has no patience with empty verbiage, postmodern relativism, hypocrisy, or pontifical certitude. My beliefs must have practical content, be in touch with an actual world with real qualities and with other humans who must live in that same world, and insofar as my beliefs are action plans, my future actions are the ultimate revealers of what I really believe. If I am willing to confess Christ with my mouth, but that confession creates no action plans with regard to my fellow human beings, then that confession is empty and hypocritical. If I affirm the validity of the Ten Commandments, but allow them to make no difference in my life, then I do not really believe them, on this account of belief. Our words are intimately connected with our actions, and as honest seekers, our words and actions should converge. None of us has it just right yet, none of us possesses accurate understandings of much of the world, so none of us possesses the complete set of best action plans. Our knowledge is as fuzzy as the unformed future that provides its content. But we can move toward that communion with the "final word," which by faith we trust to be awaiting us at the end of the journey. At that end the things we say and do will be ideally correlated to each other and to whatever kind of world houses whatever kind of selves we would be then.

Hierarchies of Habits

Using a basically Peircean understanding of belief as habit, it is possible to describe under one potentially coherent umbrella a wide variety of human endeavors that aim at finding and living the truth. Each of our lives, and our lives collectively, can be understood as hierarchies of habits engaging a fuzzy and open world. Because the world is fuzzy and open and because the future that informs the present is not a fixed and mechanical extrapolation from the past, habits are not permanent, fixed, or automatic. David Hume thought that habit and reason were fundamentally different. But Hume knew nothing of natural "habit-taking," by which new behaviors of matter could give rise to new organisms, which could then give rise to new habits, which in turn could create new habits. These processes of the self-creating world (bestowed with self-creativity by a Creator, from the Christian perspective) are quintessentially nonmechanical. They are non-linear and self-referentially fertile. So most bets are off as to where it will go from here, in detail.

A human self—you or me or any average functioning human—is the collection of millions of habits at many different levels. So let us build a self from the ground up, habit by complex habit, leaving out a few million steps along the way. Bill Cosby once performed a parody of a sports star making a television commercial for a shaving razor. The sports star would lament those "little tiny hairs, growin' out of my face." No matter what he did to them, they kept growing out every single day. Those hairs are part of a human organism. A progenitor species developed the original hair habit millions of years ago. This habit is but one of thousands of biological systems and subsystems that comprise our embodied selves. Hair has a habit of growing as long as the organism lives. Every organ in the organism has its own habits that ideally work in concert with the habits of other organs to produce the symphonic complexity of the human body. All the way down to the molecular level, matter is organized into complex patterns of complex patterns. Each of these physical patterns was started millions of years ago, and they have combined in countless different arrangements on the way to human beings, the most complex organisms.

The animals that existed prior to human beings were themselves complex combinations of habituated matter, and they carried the process of habit-taking to even more interesting and nonlinear dimensions than had their pre-animal forbears. Locomotive life developed an incredible variety of behaviors in response to its environments. These behaviors sometimes spread through populations, and culture was born. As we saw with the chimpanzees in chapter 8, different behaviors emerge as strategies for survival in different environments. Those lineages that developed the more advantageous strategies and passed them on to subsequent generations thus achieved a survival advantage over any potential competitors for resources. So physiological features that favored superior expression of advantageous culturally conditioned behaviors were selected and passed on to offspring. Potential new habits that would give shape to evolutionary descendents were thus multiplied by the millions.

At the end of the line (so far) are human beings, or *Homo sapiens*. The DNA that ensures the sufficiently habitual production of like cells from parent cells is the remarkably complex product of eons of habit-taking. Humans, much more than any less complicated species, are able to create new habits. Because of our extreme nonlinearity and complexity, we can make new habits almost at will. A simple act of will cannot keep those little tiny hairs from growing, but an act of will does seem to be able to create a family bond that will, in all probability, create children who will perpetuate some of the desired habits of the parents. A willful act apparently can initiate in the believer a habit of emulating Christ in his or her actions. We still do not have a good idea of what a "willful act" is, but at the very least it involves the instigation of a new habit, whether short- or long-lived. My life and my little portion of the world around me are different from what they would have been if my wife and I had not chosen to marry and to bring children into the world. The cultural habits of my community, and yours, are different from what they would have been if we had not followed the courses we did.

We chose our courses because our beliefs, or habits of thought, helped to determine the nature of our responses to practical future situations. Whether we think of these beliefs as the physical habits of the cerebral "wetware," or as the sum total of our convictions that give shape to our existence, matters not. From either vantage point, we all have beliefs about probably millions of things, and these beliefs are habits that steer us toward our futures and are plastic enough to adjust to crises of the unexpected. Most of these habits are lurking beneath the surface, beneath the threshold of our awareness (though Peirce preferred to speak of beliefs only as conscious). But they are there, ready to be called upon in the proper practical circumstance. Some are about small things, specific to a very limited number of potential experiences. Others are very broad, weighing in at practically every moment to help shape our approach to a huge range of choices. The broadest and deepest of all our habits, or beliefs, would ideally have an impact on every experience we have, even amid the inevitable surprises of the unknowably indeterminate future.

Just as my physiological structure is composed of systems of systems, habits that work together to form higher level habits, so my belief structure is composed of habits upon habits. At any one time the vast majority of these beliefs, these thoughts at rest, are lying in wait, ready to spring to action when needed. I may not be consciously be thinking about how I might respond to a snake crawling out from under my porch, but there is a response ready should the reptile approach. My flight from a poisonous snake is the result of a belief that it could kill me and my desire not to die. The snake-belief is but one habit among many that compose my more general habit of self-preservation. If I am healthy and my beliefs are properly arranged, the collection of habits aimed at self-preservation will itself be exercised in service of still higher-level habits. If we have a highest level habit, or belief, it is the one in service of which all of the others should exist. For Christians, this broadest level commitment might be expressed by one of the central confessions of the church, or a simpler formula, such as "to do the will of God." Ideally, this reigning belief, this habit of all habits, will be served and supported by the entire set of subsidiary habits.

For one who truly makes this habit of doing the will of God the reigning habit in his or her life, every one of the millions of sub-beliefs will support the one grand belief. Even the belief that the attraction of earth's gravity at a certain point above sea level has such and such an average value, the object of one kind of tedious measurement made by Peirce in his scientific career, can be coordinated into a larger vision or a grander belief. This is because what we learn of gravity reveals a piece of the universal puzzle. It helps us to understand everything from cosmology to proper specifications for building bridges. It helps us to understand the physics of golf ball and baseball flight, which in turn helps us to teach our children coordination, judgment, and teamwork. These kinds of connections are everywhere, and each little habit that proves worthwhile can be used in service of broader habits. We can strive to arrange all of our habits so that they work together in the service of God. With God's help, our beliefs can grow into more effective tools for building the Kingdom of God. They can work harmoniously toward the one end that really matters, and our entire selves can work in harmony with other entire selves in the production of the even higher level habits that define a cohesive community of faith.

The Guess at the Riddle

In respect to the spirit of humility and fallibilism that ought to guide all enterprises presuming to speculate about the most general nature of things, it seems fitting to close with a broad characterization of the speculations and reflections that fill these pages. They are guesses. They could be wrong. Right now the view of knowledge and reality that affirms chance and openness and uncertainty, that locates this uncertainty in the future that informs our every present moment, that interprets our embodied changeability as blessed, that sees the uncertainty that is endemic to developmental embodiedness as a friend to authentic faith, seems right to me. I cannot prove it. In an important sense this worldview is not even the conclusion of a traditionally rendered rational argument. It is a guess. The evidence cited in its support can never be more than scandalously scanty, but this is the case with any view of things that tries to be comprehensive.

Peirce reserved a very important place in his theory of knowledge for the guess. He believed that in addition to the standard modes of reasoning, deduction and induction, a third was prevalent in the practice of hypothesis formation. This third kind of reasoning he called "abduction." Peirce contended that any really new hypothesis could not be arrived at systematically by the analysis of existing data through inductive or deductive reasoning. New hypotheses, which might be ones that take us further toward the truth, must spring from an imaginative leap. The thinker must postulate a hypothesis even on the barest of evidence, essentially on a hunch. Then that hunch must be tested and tried like any other belief—in other words, the thinker who would seek to make a positive advance in understanding guesses. In Peirce's words: "Now, that the matter of no new truth can come from induction or from deduction, we have seen. It can only come from abduction; and abduction is, after all, nothing but guessing."[5] Abduction, hypothesis formation, or hopeful guessing asks the imaginative question, "If X were true, then wouldn't it cover nicely the range of experience I am trying to explain?" Then it says, "Let's postulate X, test it, and see if it works, and then see how much more it explains." If it works, then maybe the postulator is on to something. If not, then she regroups, studies the data further, and waits for another inspiration.

Peirce never published a book-length treatment of his ideas. One of the books that he intended to publish, but never finished, was to have been titled *A Guess at the Riddle*. We have ample information to understand what some of Peirce's guesses were. Some of his guesses have been presented here because they seem to work quite well so far. But his guesses and mine, yours and the Pope's, need to be tested and retested until such a time as the cooperating community of committed seekers sees eye to eye and face to face. So we test and try, hoping that all of our wrong guesses at least wind up as useful signposts on the road of inquiry. But that road is narrow, and we cannot see very far ahead, so we must keep on working out our salvation in fear and trembling, knowing that ultimately only God can bridge the gap between where we are and where we ought to be.

Notes

1. CP 5.407 (from the 1878 essay "How To Make Our Ideas Clear").
2. CP 5.311.
3. Debates about the appropriateness of scientific rationality in a multicultural world and about the nature of "advance" in the history of science are widespread and highly charged. I am weighing in here on the side of a moderate critical realism, which recognizes that human reason as exemplified in the sciences actually has made significant strides in uncovering real patterns in the universe, though that history is not without setbacks and ulterior motives.
4. CP 5.397 (from "How To Make Our Ideas Clear").
5. CP 7.219.

Index

G
Galileo, 2-3, 6, 15, 18n, 23, 61, 78
Gombrich, E. H., 22, 34n
Goodall, Jane, 151n
guess at the riddle, 35n, 160, 177-178

H
habit-taking, 74, 99, 109-114, 117-119, 128-132, 150, 159, 174-175
Heisenberg Uncertainty Principle, 52, 83-84
heredity, 48-49, 135, 141, 168
Hume, David, 7-12, 16, 56, 109, 112, 133n, 174

I
incarnation, 150
intelligent design, 124
interpretant, 31-32, 95

J
James, William, 30, 74n,
Johnson, Philip, 123

K
Kant, Immanuel, 12-15, 32, 93
Kierkegaard, Søren, 19, 66, 71, 153-159, 161-164, 165n, 171, 173
kinetic theory, 54-55

L
Laplace, Pierre Simon de, 60-62, 70, 74
leap of faith, 25, 73, 153, 157, 160, 162
Leibniz, Gottfried, 12, 61
Lestienne, Remy, 127
Leucippus, 39
Locke, John, 7-8, 12, 23

M
mathematics, 1-3, 9-11, 17, 21, 25, 61, 70-71, 74, 82, 95, 143, 156, 165n
Maxwell, James Clerk, 52, 54, 120, 122
middle-sized objects, 94-95, 100, 108
misplaced concreteness, 23-24
Monod, Jacques, 123-125
mudballs, 145, 149-151

N
natural theology, argument from design, 121, 133n
necessitarianism, 45, 47-48, 50, 62, 126, 155
Newton, Sir Issac, 50, 54, 61-62, 78, 80-81, 158
Newtonian physics, 44
Nietzsche, Friedrich, 19, 22-23, 27, 30, 33, 93, 139, 151n
nominalism, 96n, 147
nonlocality, 80, 86, 88-89

O
objectivity, 13, 153-154, 156-158, 163-164
Ockham, William of, 147
Origin of Species, 117

P
Paley, William, 121
Peacocke, Arthur, 114n, 125, 133n
Peirce, Benjamin, 44
Peirce, Charles, passim, 19, 25, 29-33, 35n, 38, 41, 44-53, 56, 57n, 60, 62-66, 69-74, 86, 90, 92, 95, 99, 108-112, 117, 122, 128, 132, 136, 138, 145-149, 153-154, 161-164, 167-168, 170-173, 176-178
Planck, Max, 52, 79-82, 88, 96
Plato, 2, 10, 18n, 19, 24, 26-30, 32, 33, 136, 142-144, 146, 147, 170-171
pragmaticism, 74
pragmatism, 30, 62-63, 74
prediction, 49, 56, 61, 72, 91, 104, 107, 158
Prigogine, Ilya, 101-102, 104, 107-110, 112, 114, 115
problem of induction, 9
Provine, William, 124
Pythagoras, Pythagoreans, 2, 26, 29